Curriculum Theory

Alex Molnar and John A. Zahorik, editors

Selecte... um Theory
Confere... -Milwaukee,
Novem...

Association for Supervision and Curriculum Development
1701 K Street, N.W., Suite 1100, Washington, D.C. 20006

Stock number: 611-77112
Library of Congress Catalog Card Number: 77-86522
ISBN 0-87120-086-4

Contents

Foreword / v
  Elizabeth S. Randolph

Introduction / 1
  Alex Molnar and John A. Zahorik

Part I. Values and Curriculum Theory / 9

1. Values Bases and Issues for Curriculum / 10
    James B. Macdonald

2. A Neo-Conservative Approach in Curriculum / 22
    Robert Allen Ubbelohde

Part II. Rational Decision Making and Curriculum Theory / 35

3. Desirable Content for a Curriculum Development Syllabus Today / 36
    Ralph W. Tyler

4. Data Curriculum Workers Need / 45
    Daniel L. Duke

Part III. Psychological Development and Curriculum Theory / 49

5. The Role of Contrast in the Development of Competence / 50
    William E. Doll, Jr.

6. Cognitive Style: Implications for Curriculum / 64
    Charles A. Letteri

7. The Therapeutic Curriculum / 70
    David C. Williams

iii

Part IV.   Classroom Practice and Curriculum Theory / 73

8. The Ethic of Practicality: Implications for
   Curriculum Development / 74
   Walter Doyle and Gerald Ponder

9. A Phenomenological Perspective on Curriculum and Learning / 81
   Bernice J. Wolfson

Part V.   Sociopolitical Analysis and Curriculum Theory / 91

10. Toward a Political Economy of Curriculum and
    Human Development / 92
    Dwayne Huebner

11. What Do Schools Teach? / 108
    Michael W. Apple and Nancy R. King

Contributors to This Book / 127

ACKNOWLEDGMENTS

All of the papers included in this volume were presented in their original form at the Milwaukee Curriculum Theory Conference held November 11-14, 1976. The Milwaukee Curriculum Theory Conference was the fourth in a series of curriculum theory conferences. The series began in 1973 at the University of Rochester, continued in 1974 at Xavier University, and in 1975 at the University of Virginia. We are indebted to the curriculum scholars who participated in one or more of the preceding conferences for their advice and support in organizing the Milwaukee Conference. Their commitment to the field and their willingness to exchange ideas, to criticize, and to face difficult questions give testimony to the vitality of curriculum theorizing. Only a few of the papers presented at the Milkwaukee Conference are presented here. We have tried to exemplify the major themes that were developed, with the knowledge that many excellent papers have been excluded because of space limitations.

Even with the encouragement and help we received from our colleagues it would have been difficult if not impossible to organize the Milwaukee Curriculum Theory Conference were it not for the willingness of Dean Michael Stolee of the School of Education, University of Wisconsin-Milwaukee, to commit substantial resources to the project.

Final editing of the manuscript and publication of this booklet were the responsibility of Robert R. Leeper, Associate Director and Editor, ASCD publications. Additional editorial and production services were provided by Nancy Olson, Production Manager, with the assistance of Elsa Angell, Patsy Connors, Teola T. Jones, and Myra K. Taub.—A.M., J.A.Z.

Foreword

This book, a collection of papers by leaders in the curriculum field, offers educators a scholarly look at current theory. The introduction provides an excellent historical perspective in addition to definitions of some of the major theories to be discussed in the book. Each of the eleven selections expands, attacks, defends, integrates, or applies one or more of these theories. The selections seem to delineate the dichotomy between the scientific and the humanistic goals of education. However, a curriculum planner should be cognizant of both theoretical positions in order to integrate them into a viable curriculum. Teachers and administrators can develop a good curriculum only if they can comprehend the rationale for and the limitations of curriculum models. The book is divided into five parts. Although each part has a common focus, each paper presents a unique viewpoint. Collectively, they comprise a comprehensive survey of current curriculum theory.

The two papers in Part I present teachers, administrators, and curriculum theorists an examination of the importance of values in curriculum work. They contrast this perspective with the current empirical emphasis on the competency based curriculum. They also compare and contrast implicit and explicit values, curriculum talk and practice, and norm forming and non-norm forming curriculum models.

Part II deals with two kinds of decision making: decisions about curriculum design and decisions about program evaluation. Educators charged with planning, implementing, or evaluating curriculum will be provided with new questions to ask about educational programs.

In Part III there are three very different perspectives of the psychological implications for curriculum theory. In the first, a discussion about contrast and open inquiry in knowledge acquisition, there is a clear differentiation between performance and competence. This distinction is more than semantic and should be noted by those designing competency-based curricula. Teaching "learning how to learn" by using cognitive styles, and a critical look at what Williams calls the "therapeutic curriculum" of self-help, consolation, and coping strategies are presented in the other two papers.

Part IV recognizes the classroom teacher as the final curriculum designer. Educators involved in staff development will find useful the two selections devoted to classroom practice. One lists teacher criteria for the practicality of curriculum innovations and the other discusses classroom environment and also teacher assumptions about education and the teacher's role in the educational process.

The final section presents two views of sociopolitical analysis. The first, a thought provoking comparison between the theories of Marx and Piaget, should be of interest to scholars in philosophy and political science. The last paper analyzes something quite different, the interactions in a kindergarten class and how these interactions are reflective of society.

Throughout the book the contributors to *Curriculum Theory* challenge us to look at the real purpose of education, whether it is to maintain the social structure as it has existed or to improve the existing structure by providing an educational environment that maximizes human potential. Several writers strongly urge us to reexamine the values implicit in our curriculum, to redefine these or other values and to make them explicit. The tension between the curricular extremes and the integration of these extremes discussed in this work are healthy signs for curriculum theory. The papers presented here should guide educators in asking meaningful questions as they continue to work with curriculum.

Elizabeth S. Randolph, *President, 1977-1978*
Association for Supervision and Curriculum
Development

Introduction

Curriculum as a specialized field was born in the early part of the twentieth century during an era of rapid change. Kliebard [1] puts the time at approximately 1918 with the publication of Franklin Bobbitt's *The Curriculum* [2] and Clarence Kingsley's *Cardinal Principles of Secondary Education*. [3] The period following World War I was marked by industrial growth, increased immigration, rapid urbanization, and technological development. These events had a profound effect on the social, economic, and political life of America. As a result school programs underwent a dramatic change. Those with power and influence demanded that school programs be utilitarian and efficient.

Bobbitt's book, the first book written on curriculum, set the tone and established the nature of the field of curriculum. Bobbitt was greatly influenced by the principles of scientific management that were being used in industry, and he set about to apply them to education. The goal of scientific management in industry was to eliminate waste and inefficiency and maximize productivity and profits. To achieve this goal time and motion studies were conducted to identify the components of various jobs. As a result of this analysis, wasteful actions could be eliminated and exact standards of efficiency established for each job. It was assumed

[1] Herbert M. Kliebard. "Presistent Curriculum Issues in Historical Perspective." In: William Pinar, editor. *Curriculum Theorizing: The Reconceptualists*. Berkeley, California: McCutchan, 1975.

[2] Franklin Bobbitt. *The Curriculum*. Boston: Houghton Mifflin Company, 1918.

[3] Commission on the Reorganization of Secondary Education. *Cardinal Principles of Education*. Washington, D.C.: U.S. Government Printing Office, 1918.

1

that with cost accounting and quality control procedures, efficient product output would be assured.

Scientific management principles applied to education meant that the student was to be treated as raw material to be processed and transformed into a product. If schools were to become as efficient and effective as factories, waste in the curriculum needed to be eliminated. Just as jobs were analyzed in industry to discover their essential features, various life activities were analyzed so that they could be taught more efficiently in schools. This process resulted in the identification of numerous discrete skills and other learnings, and the emergence of specific, detailed objectives as the first and most important decision in curriculum development.

The ideas about curriculum that Bobbitt formulated flourished and gained prominence in the following decades with the work of Ralph W. Tyler. While Tyler did not publish his well known *Basic Principles of Curriculum and Instruction* [4] until 1950, the model of curriculum planning that he developed took shape in the 1930's when he was involved in evaluating the Eight-Year Study. Tyler clarified and amplified the scientific view of curriculum that Bobbitt originated by identifying four fundamental questions concerning curriculum and instruction:

1. What educational purposes should the school seek to attain?

2. What educational experiences can be provided that are likely to attain these purposes?

3. How can these educational experiences be effectively organized?

4. How can we determine whether these purposes are being attained?

These questions, Tyler claimed, "must be answered in developing *any* curriculum and plan of instruction." [5]

The Tyler model or rationale is a conceptualization in which ends are separate from means. Decisions about objectives or ends are separate from and made prior to decisions about activities or means. The question of objectives must be resolved first, according to Tyler, because objectives "become the criteria by which materials are selected, content outlined, instructional procedures are developed, and tests and examinations are prepared. All aspects of the education program are really means to accomplish basic educational purposes." [6] To determine objectives Tyler

[4] Ralph W. Tyler. *Basic Principles of Curriculum and Instruction.* Chicago: University of Chicago Press, 1950.

[5] *Ibid.*, p. 1.

[6] *Ibid.*, p. 3.

suggests that society, knowledge, and learners be analyzed and that the objectives which result from this analysis be screened through psychological understandings and philosophical principles to provide a consistent, manageable list.

The power and impact of the Tyler model cannot be overstated. Virtually every person who has ever been in a teacher education program has been introduced to this model. It has become synonymous with curriculum work at all levels. Teachers, curriculum committees, and curriculum theorists have perceived the asking and answering of Tyler's four questions as their main task.

The pervasive Tyler model, then, embodies the "common sense" of our culture. The four decisions reflect the prevailing assumptions about people and how they should be in relation to one another. To stand outside of Tyler is to stand outside of the dominant assumptions of American culture. The rationale, however, does not allow for substantive changes in the status quo.

Though the Tyler model is the model most closely associated with the scientific view of curriculum, it is not the only one. Numerous curriculum theorists have attempted to extend and improve the Tyler model. Certainly the curriculum planning models developed by Taba [7] and Goodlad [8] can be viewed in this way. Taba developed a more explicit model than Tyler. The Taba model consisted of seven steps:

1. Diagnosing of needs
2. Formulation of objectives
3. Selection of content
4. Organization of content
5. Selection of learning experiences
6. Organization of learning experiences
7. Determination of what and how to evaluate.

Goodlad's model places greater emphasis on values as a primary curriculum decision than did Tyler's. His model consisted of three main elements:

1. Values
2. Educational aims
3. Learning opportunities.

[7] Hilda Taba. *Curriculum Development, Theory and Practice.* New York: Harcourt, Brace, and World, Inc., 1962.

[8] John I. Goodlad with Maurice N. Richter, Jr. *The Development of a Conceptual System for Dealing with Problems of Curriculum and Instruction.* Cooperative Research Project No. 45 of the U.S. Office of Education. Los Angeles: University of California, 1966.

The Tyler model and the technological line of curriculum thinking have also been extended by instructional technologists and designers. Prominent among these individuals are Gagné,[9] Glaser,[10] and Popham.[11] They attempted to make the Tyler model more specific. Popham, for example, advocates a goal-referenced model that consists of four elements:

1. Specification of objectives
2. Pre-assessment
3. Instruction
4. Evaluation.

None of the modifications of the Tyler model has appreciably altered its substance. These modifications, however, did serve to reaffirm its perceived value and worth. The structure of the disciplines' movement is another example of this phenomenon. In the 1950's individuals such as Bruner [12] and Schwab [13] were interested in reorganizing the subject matter of the schools around the structural generalizations and inquiry methods of the disciplines. Invariably the generalizations and methods were cast into a Tylerian model.

Although over 50 years have passed since the emergence of the field of curriculum, Bobbitt could not quarrel with the direction curriculum development and theory have taken. His original view of curriculum remains dominant today. That is not to say, however, that there have not been other conceptions of curriculum. The progressive education movement and Dewey's experimentalism [14] carried a different view of curriculum. Whereas Tyler stressed ends before means and a linear relationship between ends and means, Dewey viewed ends and means as integrated and dialectically related. Dewey said that ends or objectives are outcomes of activity that give meaning to and redirect future activity.

[9] Robert M. Gagné and Leslie J. Briggs. *Principles of Instructional Design.* New York: Holt, Rinehart and Winston, Inc., 1974.

[10] Robert Glaser. "Psychology and Instructional Technology." In: Robert Glaser, editor. *Training Research and Education.* Pittsburgh: University of Pittsburgh Press, 1962.

[11] W. James Popham and Eva I. Baker. *Systematic Instruction.* Englewood Cliffs, New Jersey: Prentice-Hall, Inc., 1970.

[12] Jerome Bruner. *The Process of Education.* Boston: Harvard University Press, 1960.

[13] Joseph J. Schwab. "Structure of the Disciplines: Meaning and Significance." In: G. W. Ford and Lawrence Pargno, editors. *Structure of Knowledge and the Curriculum.* Chicago: Rand McNally and Co., 1964.

[14] John Dewey. *Democracy and Education.* New York: The Macmillan Company, 1916.

Ends, he states, "are not, as current theories too often imply, things lying beyond activity at which the latter is directed. They are not strictly speaking ends or termini of action at all. They are terminals of deliberation, and so turning points *in* activity." [15] Dewey's views never seriously challenged the major line of curriculum growth, but they were not without influence. Some of Tyler's prescriptions concerning learning experiences, for example, are clearly Deweyan in nature.

Scientism is still the major approach to curriculum work, particularly in the actual planning of school curriculum, but in the past 10 years, it has been increasingly criticized and new approaches to curriculum have begun to appear.

A helpful scheme for understanding the recent state of curriculum theorizing is provided by Macdonald.[16] Using the major human interests that Habermas [17] identified, Macdonald suggests that there are three types of curriculum theory:

1. Control
2. Hermeneutic
3. Critical.

Control theories focus on practice. They provide conceptual frameworks which are intended to increase the efficiency and effectiveness of the educational process. They accept and apply technological rationality. The curriculum development process of control theorists is based on the linear-expert model or design, according to Macdonald. That is, curriculum development begins with specific goals, moves to content and learning activities, and culminates with evaluation. Control theories, then, are essentially what we have had since curriculum became a field of study. Bobbitt, Tyler, Goodlad, and others were or are theorists whose primary value position was or is control.

The criticisms that have been leveled at control theories are numerous and well known. In addition to the criticism that they are contrary to the nature of human conduct, as Dewey suggested, they have been accused of being immoral and undemocratic. That is, control theories are said to manipulate, condition, and indoctrinate learners toward ends and use means over which they have little or no influence. Control theories have also been criticized as being harmful to the learning process because they take goal setting and determining of ways to

[15] John Dewey. *Human Nature and Conduct.* New York: The Modern Library, 1922, 1957.

[16] James B. Macdonald. "Curriculum Theory as Intentional Activity." Paper delivered at Curriculum Theory Conference, Charlottesville, Virginia, October 1975.

[17] Jurgen Habermas. *Knowledge and Human Interest.* Boston: Beacon Press, 1971.

reach goals away from the learner. Still another criticism of control theories is their masking of value positions. They give the appearance of being neutral or value free, but they clearly are not.

Hermeneutic theory, the second type of curriculum theory, emphasizes ideas and thoughts. Hermeneutic theories provide new viewpoints, perspectives, and interpretations of the human condition. Through the application of conceptual frameworks from philosophy, history, moral theory, and other humanities, they attempt to lay the groundwork for consensus in the meaning of humanism. The work of Greene [18] in applying existential thought to curriculum is an example of this type of theory.

The hermeneutic theorist, in contrast to the control theorist, is interested in meaning rather than control. He or she stands back from the demands and exigencies of the school. The focus is not primarily on practical considerations; the goal of the hermeneutic theorist is the development of new interpretations and the creation of new perspectives.

Hermeneutic theory, although only beginning to appear, has already received some criticism. Because it generally does not deal with school practice, it has been criticized as being an intellectual exercise. It also has been criticized as being negative in tone. It often provides an analysis of what is wrong with current conceptions of curriculum, without suggesting what direction curriculum ought to take. That is, it sometimes opposes without proposing. Another criticism is that, like control theory, it assumes a posture of objectivity. The value positions of hermeneutic theorists, like those of control theorists, are more often implicit than explicit.

Critical theory is the third type of curriculum theory that Macdonald identifies. Critical theory deals with both perspective and practice, with both understanding and control. Critical theorists focus on the dialectical relationship between theory and practice. Their area of concern is more encompassing than that of the other two types of theorists.

The methodology of the critical theorist is critical reflection on practice and, unlike the control and hermeneutic theorists, his or her value position is always explicit. The critical theorist's value orientation is the emancipation of persons. He or she is interested in freeing persons from oppressive social structures such as economic structures, language structures, and political structures. By integrating theory and practice and by engaging in critical reflection about the relationship of the two,

---

[18] Maxine Greene. "Cognition, Consciousness, and Curriculum." In: William Pinar, editor. *Heightened Consciousness, Cultural Revolution, and Curriculum Theory.* Berkeley, California: McCutchan Publishing Co., 1974.

progress will, hopefully, be made toward human emancipation. Freire [19] is an example of this type of theorist.

Whether or not these three types of curriculum theorizing are distinct or comprehensive, they do illustrate that movement away from a narrowly technical view of curriculum is possible. The questions that arise and that the papers in this book begin to answer are where is curriculum thinking now and in what direction does it appear to be going?

The eleven papers in this book of readings are theoretical statements about curriculum rather than fully developed curriculum theories. They are organized according to the substantive domain or area of concern of the theorist. Curriculum theories carry with them certain intentions and methods, as Macdonald's analysis of types of curriculum reveals, but they also focus on a particular domain or area. The domains of the writers included in this volume are: values, rational decision making, psychological development, classroom practice, and sociopolitical analysis. Part I, Values and Curriculum Theory, deals with the nature and function of values in curriculum work. The papers contained in Part II, Rational Decision Making and Curriculum Theory, are both theoretical statements that focus on objectives, learning activities, evaluation, and other curriculum planning decisions. Part III, Psychological Development and Curriculum Theory, is a collection of papers that look at such topics as learning, development, motivation, and maturation. Part IV, Classroom Practice and Curriculum Theory, consists of papers that focus on such classroom elements as teachers, students, learning materials, and the interactions that exist among them. The last section, Part V, Sociopolitical Analysis and Curriculum Theory, contains papers that examine social, political, and economic events and how they relate to school life.

Where is curriculum thinking now? Taken together, these papers show that the curriculum field is diverse, perhaps more genuinely diverse now than ever before. Many different substantive domains and all of Macdonald's three types of curriculum interest are represented. There are numerous alternatives to control and rational decision making curriculum models.

Where is curriculum thinking going? Our speculation is that diversity in curriculum thought will increase and divisions among curriculum positions will sharpen. Further, the need for critical theory that treats perspective and practice dialectically will become more apparent. Whatever the case it does seem clear that control theories no longer define the field and curriculum theorists no longer simply react to control theory assumptions.

[19] Paulo Freire. *Pedagogy of the Oppressed.* New York: The Seabury Press, 1974.

Part I

Values and Curriculum Theory

Although they cover the same territory, the contributors to this section describe in slightly different terms the importance of values in curriculum theory.

James B. Macdonald's paper begins with a personal examination of why he chooses to be a curriculum theorist. He refutes the contention that the curriculum field is moribund. He then argues that the evaluation of curriculum talk by practitioners and non-curriculum oriented educators is distorted by their conception of practice, practice which is held in place by existing social power relationships.

Macdonald's main point is that values must be made explicit in curriculum work. He goes on to say that these values are derived from one's conception of the basic aim of education and calls on curriculum theorists to make their value commitments clear.

A neo-conservative approach in curriculum is what Robert A. Ubbelohde argues for in his paper. This should not be confused with authoritarianism or idealism, however. Ubbelohde is looking for a basis for engaging in what he calls "norm-forming communication." Norm-forming communication is communication through which educational goals and experiences can be genuinely deliberated. He sees the problems of curriculum thinking as rooted in a crisis of legitimacy.

1. Values Bases and Issues for Curriculum

James B. Macdonald

Curriculum as a field of inquiry, and curriculum theory in particular, have been said to be moribund. Moribund means "in a dying state" or, "on the verge of extinction or termination." Persons of no less stature than Joseph Schwab [1] and Dwayne Huebner [2] have pronounced this diagnosis; and it is my opinion that they should be taken seriously, that is, their assertions should be examined carefully.

What follows here is the result of a reexamination on my part (stimulated by the assertion of moribundness) of my basic formulations, assumptions, and concerns in relation to curriculum. In the process of this reexamination the fundamental problem of the value bases for curriculum and the value bases I hold in my curriculum work became important concerns for me. Thus, what follows will be a reflection upon the problems, questions, assumptions that emerged when asking myself whether "curriculum is moribund"; and the problems of and assertion of a value basis for curriculum that evolved in the process of rejecting the assertion of the moribundity of curriculum.

The first question that presented itself was — "Why be concerned about curriculum?" There are, after all, a variety of other specialities in the field of education, most of them more popular and prestigious. And, of course, the world is open to many other callings.

[1] Joseph Schwab. *The Practical: A Language for Curriculum.* Washington, D.C.: Center for the Study of Education, National Education Association, 1970.
[2] Dwayne Huebner. "The Moribund Curriculum Field: Its Wake and Our Work." Invited address, Division B, American Educational Research Association, San Francisco, April 1976.

Each of us would find a different answer to this question. My answer surprised me in some ways.

Curriculum, it seems to me, is the study of "what should constitute a world for learning and how to go about making this world." As such it is, in *microcosm*, the very questions that seem to me to be of foremost concern to all of humanity. Such questions as "what is the good society, what is the good life, and what is a good person," are implicit in the curriculum question. Further, the moral question of how to relate to others or how best to live together is clearly a critical part of curriculum.

Thus, "why be concerned about curriculum" can, for me, be expanded to "why be concerned about life." For me, the school setting is a potentially manageable microcosm of a rather unmanageable macrocosmic society. Schools lack none of the elements found in the larger context, and they do provide, for me, concrete entry points for thought and action growing out of my own experiences. Thus, for example, I have experience with politics *in* schools that gives me a concrete referent for generalizing beyond that context.

If, on the other hand, I felt that curriculum talk and work were only specific socially available roles limited in their meaning to concrete processes and situations in schools, it would hold little interest for me. It is the human intentions embodied in curriculum making, and the micro-macro relationships that bring curriculum work alive, and create processes and situations that become more than technical problems. If curriculum's only real meaning lies in schooling, then it is fundamentally a technical problem.

Thus, from my perspective, if curriculum is moribund, then society as we know it is also moribund. This view: of the decadence, disorganization, alienation, degeneration, estrangement, anomie, loss of community, etc., in modern society is a well known thread of intellectual history, especially apparent in the work of sociologists such as Weber, Simmel, Durkheim, and Tonnies (as well as de Tocqueville, Burckhart, and Nietzsche). In fact, the tradition of classical Sociology to the present day is one which casts a pessimistic pall upon human endeavors.

If, for example, we are to take completely to heart Max Weber's concern about the rationalization and bureaucratization of society in curricular terms and turn to examining the tangle of rules, policies, self-serving bureaucratic goals, rationalized testing, behavioral objectives, etc., in schools; one might come to agree about the moribundness of the field. It is however, misleading, I think, and both fruitless and destructive to focus this critique of society upon curriculum without clearly pointing out the broader intentions and meanings.

This pessimistic view comes through our intellectual tradition in the form of hermeneutic methodology. It is committed to the quest of human understanding, and it assumes a sort of "objectivity" which I believe masks basic value questions. It is a form of curriculum theorizing that is not terribly helpful.

The presently competitive antidotes to this classical academic pessimistic "objectivity" rest in two diverse but interwoven value patterns: (a) The Marxist and/or Socialist position and (b) religion. I shall return to these "answers" a bit further on.

Theory and Praxis

A second concern that arose out of my reflections was the theory/praxis problem. Curriculum talk consists of talk about both theory and praxis. It is important to keep in mind, however, that there is a necessary and desirable difference between talk and action. Talk about theory is talk about the ideational boundaries with which we are concerned in our thinking about "making a world"; whereas talk about praxis is planning talk. (Again, neither *is* praxis.) Thus, there are three critical activities inherent in curriculum: (a) talk about curriculum, (b) talk about praxis (planning talk), and (c) praxis (including talk-in-praxis).

One of the most destructive aspects of the general techno-rational and anti-intellectual ethos of American life is the idea that social action or praxis is a preemptive activity. Thus, we hear such things as "It's only talk," "Put your money where your mouth is," etc.—as if the action would have any meaning without the communication that surrounds it. As Paul Riccouer [3] remarks, talk has to be different from praxis in terms of the way talk functions in human existence.

Jurgen Habermas [4] makes a similar distinction between work and communication. When we consider Habermas' third element—power—some interesting insights emerge.

Rather than simply ask whether our actions or praxis reflect our talk in some linear hierarchical pattern, we can more fruitfully ask what the relationships between talk and action are? Thus, for example, in what ways does our present praxis distort our talk or communication? In what ways are the so-called failures of talk being translated into action—really not failures of talk, but outcomes of power realities? We have moved a long way when we can separate clearly the difference

[3] Paul Riccouer. "Work and the World." In: Hwa Yol Jung, editor. *Existential Phenomenology and Political Theory.* Chicago: Henry Regnery Co., 1972. pp. 36-64.

[4] Jurgen Habermas. *Theory and Practice.* Boston: Beacon Press, 1973.

between "that talk is impractical" and "that talk is not politically viable." In the first case there is a suggestion of the violation of reality, whereas in the latter we recognize the feasibility of the talk to be in existing, arbitrary human arrangements. Existing praxis, held in activity by power arrangements is thus quite capable of distorting the meaning and value of curricular talk.

This can readily be seen in explicit and implicit criteria applied to the evaluation of curricular talk by practitioners and/or non-curriculum oriented educators (the predominant group being psychologists). In both cases there is often the claim to be unable to understand or see the value of curriculum talk due, I believe, primarily to the distortion of thought processes brought about by work and power. As for the moribundness of curriculum, I would suggest that this conclusion results from the distortion in judgment brought about by the existing macro social praxis and power arrangements—not by the lack of potentiality, or possibility, or vitality in curriculum talk.

Thus, having justified my concerns for curriculum and having dignified the role of curriculum theory, I would like to quickly raise three sub-questions which occurred along the way.

For example, what is the prelogical or tacit ground for curriculum talk? It seems to me that we are faced with the very question posed and discussed by phenomenologists. What brackets surround curriculum talk?

There tend to be two (at least) sets of brackets that are implicit in varieties of curriculum talk. On the one hand are those, who (as I do) tend to bracket curriculum talk by the human condition—who most probably would agree or at least accept the possibility that curriculum praxis is a reasonable microcosm of the macroscopic world, and thus curriculum talk is bounded only by its concrete referents within the human condition.

An obvious disagreement is apparent, however. The tacit as pre-logical boundary for curriculum talk for many other persons would appear to be a given cultural and social definition, located in time and space in the now of social functions. Thus, this tacit bracket channels curricular talk into technical or "objective" modes, which restricts legitimate talk to planning talk, to talk about praxis. This, I believe, is what Schwab hoped to do with his emphasis on scientific examination of praxis.

This assumptive base or ground is a fundamental problem in curriculum communication. If curriculum talk is moribund, is it dying because of its tacit or prelogical bracket of meaning? Is the source of validation, the ground of validation, no longer viable? Or, has the dominant sociocultural bracket (the technical) established its truth? Is it now moribund to inquire into the human condition?

Another concern of mine asks if curriculum theory is only talk about talk, or is it also talk about work and power? Thus, are we dealing only with talk about cultural communication (such as subject matter), or do we speak about social settings and human activity also when we talk curriculum talk? Many curriculum persons would have us talk mainly about cultural communications if we are to revitalize curriculum.

I disagree, for, it seems to me that a considerable amount of legitimate curriculum theory has been talk about power and work in the schools. In fact, I find it incredibly naive to assume that curriculum talk can be limited to examining the cultural manifestation of education in exclusion from the nature of educational experience (work), and social power.

This was (or is) in fact the point of departure between the Existential and Marxist, the human consciousness and political action wings of the so-called reconceptualist curriculum theorists. This dispute, or concern, has provided an existing basis for intellectual growth and challenge among curriculum theorists.

Another way of expressing this concern is with the question "Is curriculum talk essentially descriptive or is it talk about change?" Again, we have to grant talk a legitimate role in human endeavors in order to consider this question, for it is not the same as asking whether in proto Marxist terms, curriculum theory is intended to understand schooling or to change it.

Much of the curriculum theory of the reconceptualist kind has not dealt with exhorting or recommending prescriptions for change. This may be a reaction to technical talk, which fundamentally deals with "getting things done." Nevertheless, the question remains as to whether a Marxian, or a phenomenological, or an Existential analysis of the human school condition is enough. Certainly it throws light upon our problems, and many new insights are created which could have meaning for us. But, have we completed the task of curriculum talk without dealing directly with prescriptions for schooling?

It is especially interesting to see a Marxist analysis in this pattern. This form of analysis is usually a sweeping structural critique which then fails to state its values and prescribe its remedy. As I understand it Marx was clear that the role of the intellect was to change the world not simply to analyze it.

The existential position may be equally ludicrous, since it is very difficult to understand how freedom, choice, and authentic being get translated into some sort of general objective analysis of the human condition without being in "bad faith." Or, how can we be convinced by an abstract, general, objective statement which, as a media vehicle, contradicts the substance of its position?

Another concern I have is not unrelated but can be asked in a different way. "What kinds of cultural tools are most appropriate for curriculum talk?" We have available a rather wide range of communicative tools: varying from aesthetic criticism to technological reasoning. This includes behavioral science talk, political theory orientations, phenomenological analyses, as well as a variety of philosophical approaches.

These issues or concerns have not been raised to be answered here, but to point toward a fundamental lack in curriculum theory which creates these problems. It is a failure of theorists to explicitly state the value base of their work. There is no way theorists can avoid assuming choices of value and implying them in their work. The basic choice of communication style or cultural tool, the problems, or issues dealt with —all these concerns perceive *threats to cherished values of the theorists*, and cannot be clearly formulated without acknowledgment of those values. Fundamentally, curriculum talkers (and workers) must face up to whether they are aware of the uses and values of their work and whether their values are subject to their own control.

It is clear (or seems clear to me) that many curriculum talkers and workers with a fundamentally technological orientation are not aware of their value base (thinking it to be objective and value free), nor are they aware that their values are not subject to their own control, nor do they thus show any desire to control them. It is this value-witlessness that is frightening in the technological approach, not the approach itself, since technological rationality is obviously a potential for either human good or evil.

Any person concerned with curriculum must realize that he/she is engaged in a political activity. Curriculum talk and work are, in microcosm a legislative function. We are concerned about practical affairs, but with the goal of creating the *good* life, the *good* society, and *good* persons—this direction is implicit in the very institutional fabric of schools and curriculum. Even if we wish to deschool society and eliminate any formal curriculum agenda (in which case no need for school curriculum talk and work would exist); we still must commit ourselves to whatever values we believe create good societies, lives, and persons. And, if we curriculum talkers are to understand what *we* ourselves are saying, and communicate to others, these values must be explicit.

The Aims of Education

As an area of illustration of the value foundations of curriculum talk, let us look for a moment at perhaps the most fundamental educational value commitment, that is, *the basic aim of education*. In much curriculum talk these basic aims are implicit only.

Much of our curriculum talk is replete with concerns about objectives but says very little directly about aims of education. There is, however, no way to escape a commitment to some long range goal or aim of education in any form of curriculum discourse.

Occasionally, curriculum talk will note all the possible aims, suggest that they all are valid, and then move into a discussion of objectives which does not reflect any clear rational connection between these values and these operating objectives. Curriculum theorists (and workers) have thus shown a great uneasiness about aims or basic directions.

Let us look for a moment at some major aims of education. (Remember an aim should be reflected in the construction of a curriculum environment which would maximize the attainment of that aim.) Parenthetically, I would like to suggest that talk about objectives at the curriculum level is misplaced. Objectives talk is instructional talk. At the curriculum level (the level of environment construction) the appropriate talk is about aims (directions). Three aims that appear clearly evident to me are: (a) socialization, (b) development, and (c) liberation.

Socialization, as an aim, relates to the training potential of schooling. It is the acceptance of the status-quo by definition and the replication of the present social class and role structure, ethos, and attitudinal sets by the most efficient and effective methods possible.

There are very few curriculum persons who will own up to this aim, even if it is by far the most prevalent. It is to the credit of Bloom [5] and his "mastery" disciples and Bereiter [6] that they do admit to this fundamental aim. At least one knows the values that underlie the process. Most persons working out of this value system, however, will not admit to this aim, but insist that these procedures are neutral and "in the service" of all aims. This aim is really a statement of a larger metaphor in curricular terms. It is part of the Social Mechanistic analysis —human beings should fit into the social machine as interchangeable "parts."

[5] Benjamin S. Bloom. "Mastery Learning and Its Implications for Curriculum Development." In: Elliot Eisner, editor. *Confronting Curriculum Reform*. Boston: Little, Brown and Co., 1971.

[6] Carl Bereiter. *Must We Educate?* Englewood Cliffs, New Jersey: Prentice-Hall, Inc., 1973.

Much of curriculum rhetoric has, however, been more "permissive" in tone. That is, the explicit or implicit goal or aim of education has been proposed as human development—most specifically, the development of the individual. One sees this today in the most recent fad called Moral Education. Kohlberg et al.[7] are, of course, developmentalists.

The developmental aim is an important statement of the American experiences. It reflects an organismic or biological metaphor. This metaphor found its grounding in 19th century intellectual growth (e.g., evolutionary theory) combined with American agrarian and individualistic values, among other things.

The whole developmental approach, however, in formal educational terms (i.e., school curricular construction) does not always clearly specify the values or interests that are being served. Thus, development involves the concept of an elite group (e.g., mature vs. immature or educated vs. ignorant) that knows that direction "development" must take and how to guide this process. These directions and processes are not always clear to developers and never known to the developee (since they are immature or ignorant by definition).

An interesting analogy to this education process may be witnessed in a broader context in relation to the "underdeveloped" or Third World, especially in the case of South America. Development, in this context, is a process of becoming like the advanced capitalistic countries (mainly the United States). Development, in other words, has a direct relationship to the status of the elite or advanced group, whether researchers, teachers, or economists. Maturity, in other words (for education) is defined by the "mature" members of the society as being "like us."

A third general aim, often embedded in a developmental position, is more adequately called liberation. This is a much riskier aim and is, thus, often put in developmental terms. But, essentially, it is an aim of freeing persons from the parochialness of their specific times and places and opening up the possibilities for persons to create themselves and their societies. Because one might be called a communist or something equally as derogatory and threatening (Utopian, etc.), many curriculum talkers who apparently accept this value, camouflage it in a rhetoric of developmentalism. I suggest that many of them are not willing to face up to the action implications of their values.

The point here is that it would be a great service if curriculum talkers and workers would clearly specify their aims and begin to reflect this consistently in their work. It would greatly facilitate understanding

[7] Lawrence Kohlberg and Rochelle Mayer. "Development as the Aim of Education." Harvard Educational Review 42 (4): November 1972.

in the communication process and it would provide a clear basis for dialogue and improvement of the state of the field.

Domain Values

Curriculum, however, not only has directional value problems, it has definitional value disjunction. A second major area of value concerns is those values that are best called domain values. According to Gotshalk,[8] "A domain is any well established area of human value activity that has an established and distinctive telic pattern." Curriculum certainly qualifies as a domain (and sub-domain of education). The activity of constructing a curriculum is a purposive set of actions—a telic pattern. The question remains as to what domain values reside within the activity of curriculum making. The relevance of the question is obvious, for if there is no agreement among curriculum talkers and workers concerning domain values, there can be little communication or dialogue about curriculum.

I suppose another way of asking the question is: "What are the subpoints (variables as values) that curriculum talkers and workers feel have to be dealt with?" Tyler[9] says he is satisfied after 25 years, for example, with his four basic questions about objectives, selection, organization, and evaluation. Assuredly, he also thinks *rational decisions* are the critical unit values of the curriculum domain. I personally disagree, as do some other persons, nevertheless, it would be of great value if we *could* identify our domain values (i.e., units of conception and significant variables).

In the past (within the decision making unit value) other variables have been suggested also. Decisions about (a) significance, (b) balance, (c) scope, (d) sequence, (e) integration, and (f) continuity have also been thought to be important.

But more important, with the belated discovery of the latent or hidden curriculum, the decision making unit (i.e., rational planning) becomes somewhat suspect as the critical domain value. A unit of action or activity, some aspect of the praxis of curriculum is suggested as a more critical unit than "rational decisions."

This problem again parallels broader intellectual dialogues about praxis and consciousness and signals a point of potential dialogue and

[8] D. W. Gotshalk. *Patterns of Good and Evil.* Urbana: University of Illinois Press, 1963.

[9] Ralph Tyler. "Two New Emphases in Curriculum Development." *Educational Leadership* 34 (1): 61-71; October 1976.

disputation in curriculum talk and work (what would be more funda-mental in curriculum?) that belies the moribundness of the field; and signals its intellectual vitality and its challenge in the relatedness to broader intellectual movements.

There is one sense in which we might as well close up shop in curriculum (at least any of us other than walking and talking tech-nicians). This is if one fully believes that all values are relative and that all dominance of value is a result of the strong and elite (whomever they may be) having the political and social power in their hands to impose values. If one believes this, then any social manifestation of the good life, good society, or good person is most likely a reflection of simple power—someone(s) dream for the masses. Making history the villain doesn't change the picture. If this is a true representation of educational reality, then those of us who strive for "other" values are surely mis-placed in education. We should be seeking power, and probably by any means we can get it, or, of course, we could sink into the sleeping arms of technical activity and forget the significance of values. But curriculum talk and work as an area of integrity *is moribund*, under these condi-tions. In its most general form, the pronouncement of value relativity is that "God is dead."

I challenge this conclusion. In fact "God" is very much alive. By God, I do not necessarily point toward anyone's personal idea or any person-being. I am referring to the source or ground of the religious impulse and spirit that pervades human history and activity. In this sense, it is a course that informs humanity about itself and the potential and possibility for creating. Thus, I would suggest humanity is not created in God's image, but is busily in the process of creating itself in the image of "God."

In any case, we are faced here with the acceptance of very funda-mental values which are preserved in our definitions of good (society, life, persons); this leaves us with questions about where these values come from and what are they?

Clearly, curriculum talk and work imply "goodness" by someone's definition. What is, or should be, curriculum talkers' and workers' idea of goodness? What fundamental values inform our own activity, arise out of that activity?

It is here, that I shall express what values I feel ought to undergird curriculum talk and work; I *suppose* to illustrate the point, although hopefully *to convince someone also*. Here I am afraid I am rather paro-chial, rather American in my makeup for I believe that a kind of religious socialism should be that central core. These are in other words two fundamental value questions that inform and form the human condition. They are (a) what is the meaning of human life?, and (b) how shall we live together?

To me these two vague value loadings belong inextricably together. I think any fairly adequate reading of history suggests that the major source that gives socialism its dynamic impulse and desire for bringing about progressive human betterment *is* that core of basic spiritual value found in the human religious tradition. At very least, it is where such values and concerns as justice, equality, fraternity, and liberty seem to arise and make their appearance.

This approach irritates almost everyone. Few religious people like socialism and even fewer socialists like religious people. Not only that, but to allow yourself to be identified as either "religious" or "socialist" outside either of those small minorities is likewise to risk immediate censure.

This is unfortunate, but true. Yet it doesn't change the fact, for me, that all of those persons who are revolted by either of the combination or both, are in fact blindly or unwittingly riding piggyback on these very values as the basic impetus toward betterment in western civilization— and, it is clearly so fundamental that I believe it *ought* to be seen as underlying our curricular talk and work.

We may wish to go on sounding like pragmatists and certainly hoping that people see us as nonideologists, to continue the illusion that we are socially or affluently beyond the need of ideology; but our need for fuzzing up or covering the source of our sentiments and directions does not change the reality of where these directions come from. At a curriculum theory level, of course, to admit this would be nonacademic, not reputable, or not objective enough. Somehow, at the university level, one must pretend that one creates knowledge out of nothing, with no help from the social or biographical past, the present or hoped for future. Every bit of curriculum talk and directed work is shot full of this basic value (some basic) assumption about *goodness*. The problem is we cover it up or sugarcoat it, or are really unaware of our debts. In any of these cases, we fuzz over and disconnect the value base from the topic of our rhetoric and action. Reading much curriculum theory is like pretending the writers have no *presence* in their work. Yet this "presence" is known through the work—why not make that presence the central, the integrating agent of the work rather than ghost in the machine?

This is really not the place to argue both the politics of socialism, or religion. But I should like to conclude with a few remarks about this grounding which those of you who disagree, would like to agree, or are curious, can pursue at your own leisure.

In a sense, this makes me very old fashioned and conservative for I find two basic ideas which are very old to be the cornerstone of religious socialism. These ideas or concepts are those of the *person* and *social democracy*.

I have great difficulty beginning or ending our concern for good societies, lives, or persons without the concept of the *person* as my grounding point. Further, the only meaningful social process that manages to violate personness least is what historically has become known as *social democracy*. Social democracy is, as Michael Harrington [10] so adroitly describes, the underlying socialism that has been allowed to appear in America due to Americans' unique development.

What I am proposing is a challenge to curriculum talkers and workers to explicitly profess their basic grounding values of goodness that underlie the work they do. How do they answer the questions of the meaning of human existence; and what form of living together? What do they substitute for such concerns as *persons* and *social democracy*? And if they agree with these, why is the connection between their values and their activity (whether talk or work) so vague?

Conclusion

In conclusion, the major premise of my talk is a simple but important one. It is: *that all curriculum talk and work is value based.* Further, *examination of much of our curricular talk and work often reveals a failure to clearly identify and relate the values to the work in process.* I have suggested some critical questions and some basic areas where values need to be clearly stated, and I have hypothesized that most of the "progressive" values that transcend our dominant technical witlessness, are those which are basically derived from our religious and social democratic history. This being the case we would be well advised to pronounce *these* values and work directly through them.

[10] Michael Harrington. *Socialism.* New York: Bantam Books, Inc., 1970.

2. A Neo-Conservative Approach in Curriculum

Robert Allen Ubbelohde

Apparently not much has changed in the field of curriculum since Schwab characterized it in 1969 as "moribund" and unable to "contribute to the advancement of education."[1] It appears that the field of curriculum is in much the same situation as the fabled Zen centipede immobilized by the question as to which foot it moved first when it walked. Curriculum theorists and practitioners seem unable or unwilling to move beyond partial criticism and self-reflection or to engage in the total criticism needed to establish new conceptual and methodological means for moving the field forward.[2]

The practical implications of the immobilization of curriculum theory may best be seen in the current existential situation with regard to curriculum planning and implementation. The generation of new curricular programs and the trend toward cultural pluralism within education in the United States suggest that curriculum planners and administrators have committed themselves (a) to the provision of alternative possible curricula, and (b) to the provision of cultural and thereby educational options within curricula. The rush to embrace cultural pluralism and alternative educational programs intensifies the problem of the legitimacy of any selection of curricular options made by educators. Questions can be raised as to why any one curriculum or curricular option

[1] Joseph Schwab. *The Practical: A Language for Curriculum*. Washington, D.C.: National Education Association, 1970.

[2] See, for example: Harry S. Broudy's review of *Curriculum Theorizing: The Reconceptualists* in "Book Reviews." *Teachers College Record* 77 (4): 639-41; May 1976.

ought to be considered worthwhile (that is, be accepted as desirable) and why any particular option should be selected and offered in a school as opposed to other possible options.

Since curriculum planners or implementers in the United States cannot turn to tradition or other commonly accepted ground for purposes of legitimating any particular option or curricular plan, they must turn to their bureaucratic-administrative authority in an attempt to justify a selection. That is, the justification of a given curricular selection or option in a school must be based on the politically determined bureaucratic authority/responsibility of the administrator, teacher, or school board. That this politically based authority is not adequate for the justification of curricular selections and options, even given large electoral majorities and strong leadership, should be familiar to curricular theorists and practitioners who have dealt with the response to content in social studies curricula (*Man: A Course of Study*, for example), new math curricula, reading curricula, as well as student rights and demands, and the growth of citizen involvement in educational decision making. The growing move for negotiation of curricula within teacher contracts may also illustrate this point.[3]

The crisis for the curriculum planner or administrator in the United States becomes more critical, however, when he or she turns to "curriculum theory" for guidance. The prevailing model for curriculum development in the United States—the Tyler Rationale—is itself based on an assumption of politically-based administrative or bureaucratic legitimacy for justifying a given curriculum or specific curricular option. In his rationale, Tyler claims that "It is certainly true that in the final analysis objectives are matters of choice, and they must therefore be the considered value judgments of those responsible for the school."[4] Thus, in Tyler's analysis, the justification of educational purposes or objectives is dependent upon the presupposition that administrative/bureaucratic authority is a sufficient ground for establishing the legitimacy of curricular content and thus of a curriculum.

The problem is that to base curricular legitimacy on administrative authority is to assume that politically-based administrative authority is itself accepted by the public as an adequate ground for educational decision making. The acceptance of governmental and bureaucratic authority is itself a canon of a traditional value structure which no longer

---

[3] See: Jurgen Habermas, "On Social Identity," *Telos*, No. 19, Spring 1974, for a discussion of curricular legitimacy in West Germany.

[4] Ralph Tyler. *Basic Principles of Curriculum and Instruction.* Chicago: University of Chicago Press, 1949. p. 4.

appears to have unquestioned currency in this country. The crisis in curriculum is as such related to the broader erosion of grounds for the cultural justification and communication of values and norms, that is, (a) to the absence of a preexisting commonly accepted set of cultural values *and* (b) to the absence of communication aimed at forming cultural norms.

Faced with a situation in which grounds for legitimating curricula are lacking—that is, with a situation in which neither normative nor norm-forming communication can be presupposed—a necessary question for curriculum theorists and practitioners is: Is normative or norm-forming communication possible? I believe only an affirmative answer allows us to engage in curriculum theorizing.

Although there are many theoretical and metatheoretical issues and problems inherent in this question, these difficulties can be considered only briefly here prior to outlining a neo-conservative approach to curriculum theory and practice.

Some Theoretical Issues and Problems

First, the current situation which exists as a frame of reference for discussions of curriculum and other norm related communications has been characterized by Horkheimer as involving an "eclipse of reason." [5] We live in an age of subjective reason, an age in which the possibility of objective reason has been rejected or is denied.

Caution is needed here. Since subjective is often taken to refer to the intuitions, feelings, or emotions of a particular individual engaged in intellectual pursuits, it may be assumed that objective reason can only be defined so as to deny an emotional basis for *or* an emotional element in knowing. This is not necessarily the case. Emotion, feeling, or intuition may be denied or included in definitions of either subjective or objective reason.

Subjective reason is the name given to reason that is concerned with means. That is, ends are taken for granted in subjective reason on the grounds that ends *cannot* be reasonable in and of themselves. Ends, to the extent they can be known, are viewed as means to some further ends which in turn are viewed as means.

Objective reason, on the other hand, admits that there are means which can and must be considered in terms of their efficiency and/or effectiveness as procedures for attaining ends. Ends, however, can be known and exist in and of themselves distinct from means.

[5] Max Horkheimer. *Eclipse of Reason.* New York: Seabury Press, 1974.

Accepting subjective reason, the curriculum practitioner can justify any curricular or instructional option only as a means to some end. However, the end cannot itself be justified. Accepting objective reason commits the curriculum practitioner to the proposition that both ends and means (in that order) can be and need to be justified and further that ends are themselves justifiable. Acceptance of either subjective or objective reason ought to be determined through a critical contemplation of those concepts of the person, society, and knowledge implicit in and providing support for each view.

Based on Murdoch's discussion in *The Sovereignty of Good*,[6] what is being called here subjective reason is a view that thought is real only to the extent that it is actualized in speech or action. That is, there is *no private mental life, no thought without action.* Thought, to be real, must be manifest in action and thus open to observation by others and it is the observation of speech or action by others that makes thought real. Private thought or thought which does not result in speech or action is not "real." Further, the subjective view holds that the will or self is unrelated to thought except as a motivational force. Thought is manifest in action but does not determine or direct action. It is the will or "self" which motivates action, but the will is not controlled or influenced by thought. What we have is a picture of a person with a will which determines action and is comprised of interests, passions, needs, and thought which is public but does not control the will. Thought examines the available possible choices in terms of the interests, passions, or needs which comprise the will and makes available evaluations of the probable success of possible courses of action open to choice. Thought does not influence interests themselves nor can it direct the will to make a particular choice. It is assumed that the will makes the "right" choice in that the object or state of affairs which "best" satisfies a motivating interest is chosen freely. Thought is motivated by interests in selecting what it evaluates and provides evaluations of, but the needs and interests which comprise the self are themselves taken as given and not open to change through application of thought to them.

If acceptance of subjective reason necessitates the acceptance of the view of the person described earlier then it follows that rejection of this view of the person provides *a* basis for the rejection of the subjective view of reason.

In the subjectivistic notion of personhood, guilt or duty (among other moral concepts), appear to be meaningless concepts. Insofar as will chooses that which fulfills an interest, the choice must be right even

---

[6] Iris Murdoch. *The Sovereignty of Good.* New York: Schocken Books, 1970.

though the need itself is not good or the choice does not satisfy the motivating interest. Yet, people do feel guilty and people are thought to be guilty or wrong for having certain interests and/or for behaving in certain ways.

Thus, not only does the subjectivistic view of humanity make the discussion of a variety of virtues meaningless but given this view the conception of a growing depth of understanding of a virtue is impossible. *Love,* for example, must of necessity be reduced to the fulfillment of some (sexual) interest or need and except to the extent that sexual acts may be more or less fulfilling (*enjoyable*), there is no ground for talking of a deepened understanding of love.

Despite the historical ascendancy of subjective reason, it seems unlikely that individuals (especially educators) will agree to the notion that their understanding of moral concepts such as love does not increase and deepen over time or to the notion that increased understanding cannot lead to the reformulation of an interest or need. This would explain attempts by theorists to move beyond self-interest as it is presented in the subjectivistic view of the *person* by moving on to a consideration of the *community,* the *social order* taken as a whole. Consideration of the greater good or interests of the community has been undertaken as a means for rescuing at least some of the values and moral concepts needed for political association (if nothing else) which disappear given the subjectivistic view of the person.

The view of society or community which is put forward on the subjectivistic view of reason is essentially a contractual one.[7] Given the competing interests of individuals freed from the compulsion of objective reason by which to mediate *and* resolve disagreements, means for resolving disagreements and regulating competing self-interests is necessary. The notion of enlightened self-interest and the regulation of interests by actual or presupposed contractual agreements offers an alternative both to the anarchical chaos threatened by unbridled self-interest of "free" individuals in open and free competition and to the autocratic imposition of the interests of one person or a small group of people.

The assumed motivation for accepting a contractual agreement by self-interested individuals is the notion that self-preservation (a presupposed interest of individuals) is possible only insofar as group preservation is possible. Of course, certain types of individual interests (life and pursuit of individual happiness, for example) are recognized as inalienable. Government thus serves the function of adjudicating dis-

---

[7] See: Pitirim Sorokin. *The Crisis of Our Age.* New York: E. P. Dutton & Co., 1941.

agreements resulting from conflicts of interests and of ensuring the basic freedoms of individuals to fulfill interests.

It is noteworthy that neither normative nor norm-forming communication is a prerequisite for nor a function of the contractual community. In fact, the determination of values and norms insofar as this consists in the satisfaction of interests by individuals is assumed to be an inalienable right of individuals in free and open competition. The separation of church and state and the rejection of the idea that schools ought to teach values are reflections of this rejection of the norm-forming and normative functions of the secular community. Thus, on the subjectivistic view of community, social organization and cooperation is neither viewed as valuable in itself nor involved, therefore, in the determination of individual or group interests.

In short, the social group as it is construed within a subjective view of reason is not able to replace the loss of objective values with socially constructed values. The *possibility* of a norm-forming community does not exist and normative communication based on the acceptance of (as opposed to formation of) intersubjective values and norms is absent on a subjective view of reason.

Finally, one of the philosophical presuppositions *and* outcomes of the subjectivistic view of reason is the assertion that knowledge of the good is impossible. This conclusion is often stated as what has come to be known as "the naturalistic fallacy" as defined and discussed by G. E. Moore among others. What is often ignored in considering the "naturalistic fallacy" (the notion that *ought* claims cannot be derived from *is* claims) is that at least for G. E. Moore there were two questions for consideration: (a) Is *the* good definable?, and (b) Is *good* definable? Thus, although Moore argues that *good* is indefinable, he claims that *the* good is definable. Put simply, an action, object, or state of affairs to which we apply the adjective "good" may give us pleasure, be profitable, win approval of others, be harmonious, and so forth. The fact that we experience pleasure, profit, approval, harmony, or something else from an action, object, or state of affairs, however, does not make it good. It may be true that a good act is also always pleasurable, but it does not follow that a pleasurable act is necessarily a good act. Thus, we cannot inductively define the adjective *good* by deriving a meaning from what *is* the case. We must know what *the* good is if we are to call an act, object, or state of affairs *good*. *Good* is not, therefore, a property of objects, actions, or states of affairs but depends upon knowledge of *the* good for its meaning. While it is impossible herein to explicate Moore's position and expand upon it, it can be noted that much of the *Principia*

however is the notion that persons have different *interests* due to class, race, sex, and so forth, which prevent intersubjective, norm-forming communication. Further, cultural pluralism is typically proposed as the acceptance of the legitimacy of these varied interests. Given the assumed irreconcilability of interests, the argument for cultural pluralism typically holds that lacking standards of value beyond group and personal interests, the differences which exist in behavior aimed at the fulfillment of interests ought also to be accepted. Cultural pluralism is as such an argument for radical value relativism. To reject this position does not entail intolerance, however. To argue that knowledge of the good is possible and that *the* good is the same regardless of individual or group interest does not entail the actual or psychological extermination of those whose behavior or understanding is at variance. It is true that the position being taken assumes that certain sorts of behaviors—specifically those behaviors which negate or reduce the possibility of norm-forming communication, such as intolerance itself—will not be accepted on objective reason.

Curriculum theorists and practitioners of a neo-conservative stripe then must be committed *not* to a set of norms but rather to norm-forming communication itself as a norm.

In suggesting the assertion of norm-forming education as a value by curriculum theorists, another "neo-conservative" assumption needs to be made explicit, namely, the assumed worth of each person as a free moral agent (as opposed to the radical independence of people). It is assumed that each person is capable of "vision" and that *the process of communal formulation of norms* must take into account each individual's understanding and worth as an end in him- or herself. Rather than reassert the radical *freedom of interests* which is common to conservative, liberal, radical (including Marxist), and reactionary thought today, the desire for and capability of each person with regard to insight must be assumed and the moral freedom of persons as ends must be redefined in terms of increasing individual and group freedom from fantasy (whether this fantasy be, for example, of a sexist, racist, religious, professional, or class nature). Freedom is a cooperative struggle in which "we" must replace "I" without denying the worth of the "I." This is not to deny either the "psychological" or "historical" individuality of persons as actors or learners, it is to deny that historical and/or psychological identity determines moral truth or prohibits norm-forming communication (that is, community).

A neo-conservative position is democratic in aim, but assumes that democratic dialogue itself presupposes a commitment to norm-forming communication as a shared value. Since the revitalization or resurrection of a contractual form of democratic governance seems both theoretically and practically impossible, a reexamination of democratic governance seems necessary. Democracy can be viewed as motivated by a shared vision of the worth of participation in norm-forming communication itself. This is the model which motivated the town meeting—often taken as an example of "pure" democracy in action. That is, if our understanding of democracy is stripped of contractual notions related to the individualistic pursuit of self-preservation and self-interest and if democracy is redefined in terms of the necessary worth of norm-forming communication (the struggle for consensus), then the neo-conservative position being outlined here is a reaffirmation of democratic governance.

Methodological implications follow from these assumptions. If it is assumed that a primary goal or purpose of education is to prepare students for participation in democratic, consensual, norm-forming communication, it must be assumed that schools will utilize consensual methods of norm-forming communication as the primary method in education. While development of the ability to *see the* good and training in basic skills are necessary educational goals, one of the assumptions inherent in a neo-conservative approach is that institutions and methods themselves can be judged as to their inherent reasonableness in light of a shared vision of *the* good. That is, the educational goal of bringing into being norm-forming communication entails that educational methods be such as to bring this about. Methods which prevent or work to deny the possibility of norm-forming communication must be rejected. Dialogue (discussion aimed at forming norms), as treated by such writers as Freire and Buber, must characterize educational methodology, it would seem, as opposed to the monological methods, that is, methods aimed at controlling thought and behavior, proposed by writers such as Skinner, Dewey, or Bruner. In short, methods which operate to prevent norm-forming communication within educational institutions are inappropriate and unreasonable.

To the extent that students have been conditioned by existing educational practices to respond to externally imposed stimuli, a necessary first step in education is an unconditioning process such as that described by Carl Rogers in *Freedom To Learn*.[10] By confronting students with their freedom, their worth as moral agents, it may be possible to lead persons back to self-initiated, self-directed, and self-sustained learning. This entails, perhaps, a certain amount of initial dissatisfaction on the

[10] Carl Rogers. *Freedom To Learn*. Columbus, Ohio: Charles E. Merrill Publishing Co., 1969.

part of students and chaos, such as noise, disruptive behavior, and aim-lessness, in a classroom as a teacher refuses to direct or assign individual tasks and dispense rewards.

A Rogerian approach, however, is not sufficient in itself to lead to norm-forming community, since the Rogerian approach is itself based in a subjectivistic notion of the radical "freedom" of individuals each with his or her own needs, interests, and desires.

Thus, given a desire to learn and increased ability to direct their own learning, students will need to be taught how to engage in group-based investigation. The *desire* to participate in learning with others probably does not need to be taught, however, the human relations skills and necessary values of tolerance, patience, and honesty do need to be developed. The group investigation method as developed by Thelen is a strategy which suggests itself here.[11] In the Thelen model, the teacher aims at teaching the skills and values necessary for group related in-vestigation. Although content may vary by group, individuals within any particular group develop further group discipline and skills. The value of a model of learning such as Thelen's is that it combines intel-lectual discipline with reflection on group process. An outcome of the Thelen model should be the acquisition of a commitment to group investigation (norm-forming communication) as something desirable in itself.

Both Rogerian and group investigation procedures, however, must be understood in terms of the relationship between teacher and student and between student and student. Here, Freire's position as explicated in *Pedagogy of the Oppressed* [12] is instructive as are Buber's ideas.[13] In Freire's view, there are certain values and attitudes, such as faith, hope, and love, which must permeate the relationship between or among per-sons. Further, there must be an object of reflection which may be a book, idea, picture, or state of affairs to mediate the relationship. It is not the teacher's presuppositions about the "object" but the object itself which provides the basis for discussion and inquiry. Initially, a teacher may need to select and present objects for reflection until the group can take group responsibility for such selection. This is a process of thematic investigation described by Freire as the basis for selecting appropriate objects for individual or group reflection.

[11] Herbert A. Thelen. *Classroom Grouping for Teachability.* New York: John Wiley and Co., 1967.

[12] Paulo Freire. *Pedagogy of the Oppressed.* New York: Herder and Herder, 1968.

[13] Martin Buber. *I and Thou.* Walter Kaufman, translator. New York: Charles Scribner's Sons, 1970.

Ultimately, the aim of Freire's and Buber's position is dialogue (norm-forming communication) between teacher-learner and learner-learner. This is learning focused on a common object of reflection and carried out in recognition of the participants' moral worth as ends in themselves. The Socratic dialogues of Plato present at least a rough approximation of what learning and teaching might look like. Advanced seminars held on a topic of mutual concern for participants may also suggest a model here.

It might be well to note here that moving from a Rogerian to a teacher-directed group inquiry model and from there to a collegial discussion model as sequential instructional methods may gain some support from developmental psychology. To the extent that human development moves from an egoistic to social orientation, from concrete to formal reasoning process, or from self-centered to principle-based morality, teaching practices might be altered to reflect the stages of development. Further, the teaching methods outlined earlier share a concern for the treatment of each person as an end in him- or herself.

Conclusion

While much needs to be done to explore further a neo-conservative approach in curriculum, it should be apparent that the hope expressed herein is neither a hope for the resurrection of the "absolute" in whatever form (Thomistic, Marxian, Hegelian) nor the hope for an authoritarian political regime based on a flight to such an absolute. Fascism based on a conservative absolutistic idealism is as much to be abhorred as a liberal-democratic-proletarian dictatorship based on an absolutistic value relativism. A neo-conservative approach must be constructed on the assumption of the worth of all individuals as human beings not on the reaffirmation of the individual pursuit of self-interests. A neo-conservative view must be based on the assumption that norm-forming community is desirable as well as possible and that it is a prerequisite for individual freedom. Self-preservation as a goal must be replaced by norm-forming community as a goal—the "I" must be replaced by the "we." This view is "conservative" in that it reaffirms the conservative notion of the possibility of acquiring knowledge of *the* good and in reaffirming the inherent worth of individuals, past, present, and future. A neo-conservative view is democratic with regard to consensual participation as opposed to majority rule but does not entail or presuppose a contractual agreement. Contractual agreement must be replaced by a respect for persons and the realization that even preservation, self or group, presupposes a commitment to norm-forming communication as good in itself.

Finally, it is assumed in a neo-conservative view of curriculum that the good can be known and that the function of education, in the tradition of Plato and Aristotle, is to produce good citizens.

Part II

Rational Decision Making and Curriculum Theory

The two papers in this section have a control orientation. Ralph Tyler reaffirms his contention that his four steps are basic to the curriculum development process. He adds two new areas of concern to his earlier work: the active role of the learner and the importance of out-of-school learning. In each case however, these concerns are contained within the framework of his four steps.

Daniel Duke is concerned that curriculum workers do not have an adequate data base for making curriculum decisions. He argues that systematic data gathering is not currently the basis for curriculum change and urges that investigations be undertaken by practitioners and curriculum workers in collaboration.

Throughout his text Duke equates curriculum with content and expresses his belief that the primary obstacle to course improvement is insufficient information.

3. Desirable Content for a Curriculum Development Syllabus Today

Ralph W. Tyler

When I was invited to speak on this subject at this conference, I assumed that the topic referred to the syllabus I prepared more than 25 years ago for a course I offered at the University of Chicago, and that I was being asked how such a syllabus would differ under the circumstances of today. Most of what I have to say is based on this assumption.

A Comprehensive Syllabus

The term syllabus is applied to several kinds of guides for courses or programs. Some are in outline form without extended comments or explanations; others, like the one I prepared in 1949, are in the form of expository discourse. Whatever the form, a syllabus sufficiently complete to guide student learning might well include:

1. A statement of the reason for offering the course or program; for example, for whom it is intended, what values it is likely to have for these students, and how it is related to other courses or programs

2. What the educational objectives are; that is, what students will be helped to learn

3. For each division or unit of the course or program, a statement or listing of the learning tasks that are provided

4. A suggestion of the time probably required to perform the tasks successfully

5. The means that will be used to evaluate the student's performance

6. Whatever else is necessary for the particular course or program to guide students in utilizing effectively the resources available for their learning.

In brief, a syllabus should serve as a published guide to help students in selecting a course or program and in carrying on successfully the educational activities. The preparation of such a syllabus helps the instructional staff to identify unsettled issues regarding purposes and means, and requires thoughtful consideration and operational decisions to clarify learning goals and establish the student learning system.

As I reviewed the earlier syllabus, I found no reason to change the basic questions it raises. What should be the educational objectives of the curriculum? What learning experiences should be developed to enable the students to obtain the objectives? How should the learning experiences be organized to increase their cumulative effect? How should the effectiveness of the curriculum be evaluated? These are still basic and their importance has been reaffirmed by the experiences of the past quarter of a century. However, some changes of emphasis are necessary and I want to comment on two of them.

I would give much greater emphasis now to careful consideration of the implications for curriculum development of the active role of the student in the learning process. I would also give much greater emphasis to a comprehensive examination of the nonschool areas of student learning in developing a curriculum.

Overlooking the Learner's Active Role

In the massive curriculum projects of the 1960's in the United States, the objectives were usually selected by subject matter specialists with little attention given to the needs and interests of the learners. Mention was most often made of the "educational delivery system" as though education could be delivered to students rather than their having to acquire it through their active learning. Educational technology was commonly treated as though it was the robot teacher rather than furnishing certain tools that teachers could employ as, for example, presenting material that could be used as part of a learning experience. Some of the projects actually sought to develop "teacher-proof materials." These terms and the attitudes they represent indicate that some leading curriculum builders are overlooking the fact that learning is a process in which the learner plays an active not a passive role. It is the behavior that the learner carries on with consistency that can become part of his or her repertoire of behavior and, in this way, will have been learned.

Human beings cannot be forced to learn intellectual and emotional behavior. Only under coercion or when offered tempting rewards will they even attempt a learning task which seems to them meaningless or distasteful, and even then if their experiences with the task are not rewarding, they will not continue the behavior and it is not learned. Furthermore, the behavior becomes a permanent part of their repertoire only if they continue to carry it on. This means that learners must see the way in which the things they learn can be used, and they must have the opportunity to continue to employ the learned behavior in the various situations they encounter.

Implications in Selecting Objectives

These conditions for learning have important implications to consider in selecting educational objectives. The curriculum objectives selected should not only be (a) important things for the students to learn in order to participate constructively in contemporary society, (b) sound in terms of the subject matter involved, and (c) in accord with the education philosophy of the institution, but also they should be of interest or be meaningful to the prospective learners, or capable of being made so in the process of instruction. This criterion is mentioned and briefly developed in the earlier book, but it is being overlooked even by some whose curriculum development rationale appears to be similar.

This does not imply that the interest of learners and their understanding of the meaningfulness of educational objectives at any given time are permanent and do not change. Quite the contrary, in a particular unit of study although the initial objectives should be those that students at the time see are interesting and/or meaningful things for them to learn, as they go through the learning experiences they will broaden and deepen their interests. As they gain greater understanding of the relevance of what they are learning, they will see the meaning of and develop interest in objectives that stimulate them to further study. For example, a child who has not been read to by parents and who has not seen others enjoying reading is not likely to participate actively in decoding exercises in a primary reading program nor is the child likely to see that they have any meaning for him or her. The appropriate initial objectives in reading may be those that help this child find fun in material that is read to him or her. Then, the child will want to read some of these materials, too. The objectives then can reflect these new interests the student has acquired.

Implications in Designing Learning Experiences

These conditions for learning are also important to keep in mind in the design of learning experiences. If students are to enter wholeheartedly into the learning, they should perceive what the behavior is that they are expected to learn and feel confident that they can successfully carry through the learning tasks. If they are uncertain about what they are expected to learn and lack confidence in their ability to carry on the learning task, they will balk, stumble, or openly avoid trying. They do not want to make fools of themselves or fail in their efforts. Hence, well-designed learning experiences will show learners clearly what they are expected to learn, and will employ learning tasks that are within their present abilities to carry through. As they succeed in their initial activities and gain satisfaction from their efforts, the learning tasks should be increasingly demanding in difficulty or in higher levels of attainment. This means that the sequential organization of learning experiences is developed in terms of the progress learners can make in undertaking successively more varied and more difficult learning tasks. Sequences that are designed solely in terms of the logic of the discipline are not likely to be effective in meeting these conditions for learning.

The Learner's Role in Transfer of Training

The failure to transfer what is learned in school to situations outside of school is a problem that has long been central to educational psychologists. Schools are established to help students to acquire behavior that is important for constructive out-of-school activities. If something is learned in school that is not used by the student in relevant situations outside of school, most of the value of the learning has been lost. This appears to be happening in some of the current educational programs. For example, the National Assessment of Educational Progress in 1972-73 conducted an assessment of mathematical knowledge and skills. The 17-year-olds completed computations using integers, fractions, decimals, and percents. Over 90 percent correctly answered the addition, subtraction, and division problems involving whole numbers. The percentage was slightly lower (88 percent) for multiplication. Most 17-year-olds can compute correctly. However, the percents are much lower on exercises involving simple uses of mathematics. As an example, only 34 percent of the 17-year-olds answered correctly the following:

"A housewife will pay the lower price per ounce for rice if she buys it at the store which offers

12 ounces for 40 cents

14 ounces for 45 cents

1 pound 12 ounces for 85 cents

2 pounds for 99 cents."

On other similar tasks involving other products, the results were about 46 percent correct responses. In contrasting this to the 90 percent correct responses on computation exercises, it seems probable that many students were following a curriculum that has been emphasizing drill on computation at the expense of practice in using mathematics in the situations common to contemporary life. Learning experiences can be designed that involve many situations like those outside of school, and students can be encouraged and asked to use what they are learning *in* school in relevant situations they encounter *outside* of school. The advice to schools now frequently heard, "Get back to basics," is being so narrowly interpreted that the importance of transfer of training is forgotten.

The results of the National Assessment are not the only indications that the objectives and learning experiences of some educational programs fail to interest and actively engage many students in learning and do not carry over beyond the school environment. Interviews with high school graduates and dropouts indicate that a majority cannot recall many subjects in which they learned things that would be helpful to them in later life. Clearly, the curriculum rationale should strongly emphasize giving serious attention in curriculum planning to the interests, activities, problems, and concerns of the students. Where possible and appropriate, the students themselves should participate in the planning and evaluation of the curriculum.

Examining the Non-School Areas of Student Learning

Another needed change in the emphasis of the book is a greater recognition that the school curriculum is only part of the educational experiences needed by children and youth if they are to acquire the interests, attitudes, knowledge, skills, and habits that can enable them to participate constructively in a modern society and to use their talents fully in contributions both to society and to their own personal fulfillment. The total educational system required today includes much more than the school. What young people experience in the home, in their social activities in the community, in the chores and jobs they carry on, in the religious institutions where they participate, in their reading, in their listening to radio and viewing of TV, and in the school, are all included in the actual educational system through which they acquire knowledge and ideas, skills and habits, attitudes and interests, and basic values. The school is an important part of this educational system in furnishing the opportunity to learn to read, write, and compute, and to discover and use the sources of facts, principles, and ideas that are more accurate, balanced, and comprehensive than are provided in most homes, work places, or other social institutions. The school also supplements and complements learning furnished by the other institutions, and is usually an environment which more nearly represents the American social ideals than the larger society. In most schools, each student is respected as a human being without discrimination, the transactions in the classroom are guided by an attempt to be fair and dispense justice, and the class morale is a reflection of the fact that the members care about the welfare of others.

In educational systems of the past, the several parts have certain interdependent features. The student's interest in learning what the school sought to teach was usually stimulated in other parts of the system, in the home, in the working place, and in the social life of the community so that the school did not need to develop particular motivation for learning on the part of the majority of students. Furthermore, as mentioned earlier, as skills in reading, writing, and arithmetic were developed in the school, the student found many opportunities for their use in his or her activities outside the school, particularly in work and in recreation. Skills quickly become inoperative when their use is infrequent. If the only reading required of youth is that assigned in school, reading skills do not reach a mature level. If writing is limited to an occasional note or letter, writing skills remain very primitive. If arithmetic is not used in such home activities as consumer buying, furniture construction, and budgeting, arithmetic skills and problem-solving techniques are likely to be inadequate. Hence, the total educational system needs to be viewed as one in which practice as well as initial learning is provided.

The fact that an adequate educational system in a modern society must include experiences outside the school where young people spend most of their time, combined with the fact that, while the time available to the school has remained relatively constant, the time given to education by parents, community agencies, and work settings has been greatly reduced, has several implications for curriculum development.

Educational Objectives for the School

The school curriculum should give stronger focus to the important objectives that can be learned in school, making use of the specialized resources the school provides—teachers with training in the fields of scholarship, books and libraries, laboratories and shops, a humane tradition which encourages openness, trust, and a concern for others, and an environment where order and composure are possible. The contributions that can be made to young people by helping them learn to use these resources are not minor. A world beyond their direct experience can thus be opened to them and they can develop aspirations, styles of life, skills of accomplishment more varied and more individualized than the typical limited patterns their own community affords.

The Out-of-School Curriculum

A second implication is that school leaders, particularly curriculum specialists, should work with the other community leaders to reestablish an effective educational system at the community level. The public can be helped to recognize that an adequate education for their children and youth requires an effective educational system which includes the school but also depends on experiences provided outside the school. The community should be responsibly organized to provide comprehensive educational opportunities for young people. This means that some form of community council or board is necessary to assess educational needs, identify actual and potential resources (including the schools), and to develop the outline of educational programs to meet the needs identified. These community councils or boards should direct attention to the development of resources that will require little or no additional expenditures. It seems unlikely that a free society can levy the taxes required to furnish paid professionals to fill the gaps created by the erosion of our earlier educational system. The Soviet Union has been able to support the Young Pioneers and the Communsol, which are part of school educational agencies, through compulsory levies. Doubling the tax rate for education in the free societies is unlikely to achieve public support. The curriculum for the comprehensive educational system will also need to be developed.

A third implication is that the school should help its students deal constructively with the out-of-school environment. The school can help young people develop skill in evaluating mass media, particularly TV and the press, and in finding and choosing programs and publications that are helpful and satisfying. Since the viewing of television represents for many young people the major use of their waking hours, the development of knowledge, skills, attitudes, interests, and habits that will increase the value of this activity is very important. The school can also furnish opportunities both formal and informal for students to reflect upon the significant out-of-school experiences they are having and seek, through discussion, to clarify the consequences of their actions, and to formulate meaningful standards to guide them in these transactions.

The Community as a Resource

It is also possible, even where no community educational council exists, to work with other community agencies in providing opportunities for what the National Association of Secondary School Principals (NASSP) calls "Action Learning." Action learning may be in paid form or in non-paid volunteer work with private, public, or community service agencies. NASSP has published a report on 25 action-learning schools.[1] A more extensive collection of concrete illustrations of existing programs that have enabled young people to participate in productive adult activities and to assume real responsibility for what they do is a book, *New Roles for Youth in School and Community*,[2] prepared by the National Commission on Resources for Youth. These reports furnish evidence that some schools, at least, can develop a curriculum that vitalizes and strengthens the educational experiences developed outside their walls.

In Summary

Many curriculum projects of the last two decades have overlooked the active role of students in learning and have assumed that they can be made to learn. They have given little or no attention to the interests, concerns, and perceptions of the students in developing the curriculum. Hence, it seems necessary to give special emphasis to the implications of the learner's active role when selecting objectives, developing learning experiences, and designing their sequences.

It is also clear that there is a great erosion taking place in the total educational system in America. The home, the working place, the religious institutions, and the educational milieu of the community are

[1] National Association of Secondary School Principals. *25 Action Learning Schools.* Reston, Virginia: NASSP, 1974.

[2] National Commission on Resources for Youth. *New Roles for Youth in School and Community.* New York: Citation Press, 1974.

furnishing fewer constructive learning experiences for young people than was true in the past. It is particularly necessary now in curriculum development to give careful consideration to the non-school areas of student learning. In some cases, the school can help to establish a more constructive total educational system. It can always seek to maximize the effectiveness of the school curriculum in relating to the other learning experiences of the student.

4. Data Curriculum Workers Need

Daniel L. Duke

It is this writer's contention that curriculum researchers have abandoned classroom realities—the exigencies of instructional method and student learning—to educational psychologists and retreated into a narrow realm populated by curriculum developers, political polemicists, and epistemologists. The time is overdue for curriculum researchers to cultivate perspectives on the concerns of teachers that will balance, if not offset, the psychological points-of-view that have dominated the study of classrooms for the past half century.

How to modify, update, and otherwise improve existing curricula is a concern shared by virtually all teachers, not to mention supervisors and curriculum coordinators. Those who study curriculum in universities, however, have devoted little time and energy to collecting data and developing techniques that might facilitate the annual process of course improvement. Irene Muzio, Lauri Wagner, and I have been working at Stanford and in Bay Area schools to refine methods for obtaining the kind of information that can assist practitioners in making curriculum decisions.[1] These methods are grouped under the rubric "instructional audit."

A detailed rationale for the audit has been presented elsewhere.[2]

[1] A detailed report on five field studies of the instructional audit will be forthcoming in a volume to be published under the auspices of the Hoover/Stanford Teacher Corps Project and the Center for Educational Research at Stanford.

[2] Daniel Linden Duke. "The Instructional Audit—A Comprehensive Approach to Course Improvement and Classroom Research." A presentation made at the Milwaukee Curriculum Theory Conference, November 1976.

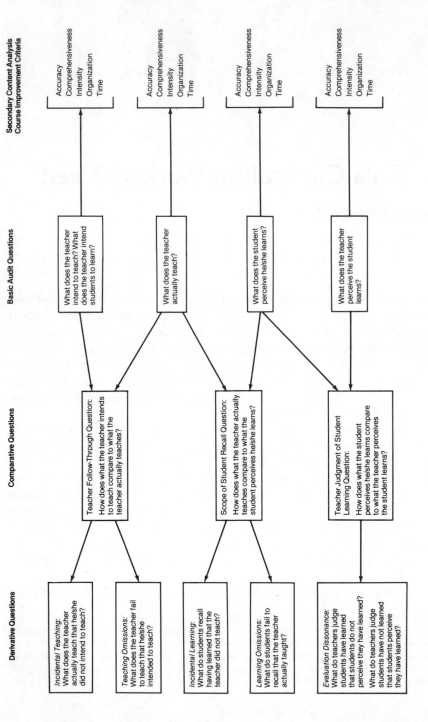

Secondary Content Analysis
Course Improvement Criteria

Accuracy
Comprehensiveness
Intensity
Organization
Time

Accuracy
Comprehensiveness
Intensity
Organization
Time

Accuracy
Comprehensiveness
Intensity
Organization
Time

Accuracy
Comprehensiveness
Intensity
Organization
Time

Basic Audit Questions

What does the teacher intend to teach? What does the teacher intend students to learn?

What does the teacher actually teach?

What does the student perceive he/she learns?

What does the teacher perceive the student learns?

Comparative Questions

Teacher Follow-Through Question: How does what the teacher intends to teach compare to what the teacher actually teaches?

Scope of Student Recall Question: How does what the teacher actually teaches compare to what the student perceives he/she learns?

Teacher Judgment of Student Learning Question: How does what the student perceives he/she learns compare to what the teacher perceives the student learns?

Derivative Questions

Incidental Teaching: What does the teacher actually teach that he/she did not intend to teach?

Teaching Omissions: What does the teacher fail to teach that he/she intended to teach?

Incidental Learning: What do students recall having learned that the teacher did not teach?

Learning Omissions: What do students fail to recall that the teacher actually taught?

Evaluation Dissonance: What do teachers judge students have learned that students do not perceive they have learned?

What do teachers judge students have not learned that students perceive they have learned?

Table 1. Outline of an Instructional Audit

The audit's basic premise is that *what* is taught is as important in the teaching-learning process as *how* it is taught. Unfortunately, much recent educational research has concentrated so exclusively on teaching methods and learning processes that the impression has been created that content is relatively unimportant. Curriculum researchers have done little to dispel this impression. They have tended to focus on what teachers *intend* to teach rather than on what actually is taught.

The audit involves recording what is taught during a typical curriculum unit (or any one to two week period). Data also are collected on what the teacher intended to teach, what students perceive they learned, and what the teacher perceives students learned. The auditor must note all learning items introduced during the unit, including board notes and handouts. The overall collection of data is guided by a series of related questions and course improvement criteria (see Table 1).

Once an audit is finished and the data have been gathered, several processes can take place. If the teacher desires a clearer understanding of the comprehensiveness of the subject matter coverage over a period of time, the teacher can request that the data be analyzed in terms of specific learning items. The auditor, who can be a colleague or a specialist, serves as the teacher's personal consultant. The auditor might classify course content into categories such as the following: facts, concepts, rules, explanations, feelings/attitudes, and skills. The teacher can study the breakdown of the learning items covered during the audit and become aware of the *range* of content with which he/she was dealing. Frequency counts of learning item categories indicate how much of each type of learning item was introduced.

Some teachers might desire information about the relationship between instructional *time* and curriculum *organization*. Audit data permit them to answer questions such as the following: Does a relationship exist between student learning and (a) the number of times a learning item is introduced in class or (b) the total amount of time spent on a learning item?

Other teachers might wish some knowledge of their instructional effectiveness as it relates to particular course content. In the past the typical approach to determining teacher effectiveness has involved comparing teacher X using method A to teacher Y using method B, with some effort to ensure relative comparability among students. The audit, however, allows teacher X using method A to be compared to teacher X using method B. In other words, an individual teacher can gain an understanding of his/her most effective instructional methods by comparing the audit data with the post-audit student achievement information.

If curriculum researchers are to demonstrate that their skills and insights are relevant to the daily enterprise of schooling, they must cease regarding content apart from the context of classroom instruction and student learning. I have suggested three uses to which audit data can be put in an effort to improve professional competence. Other possibilities exist. Audit data can be employed to assist teachers in assessing their content accuracy, determining how students reconstruct what they learn in class, and judging the level of detail accorded specific learning items. Field studies conducted over the past year also suggest that the audit provides teachers with a convenient and systematic way to look at the relationship between curriculum content, instruction, and learning.

Part III

Psychological Development and Curriculum Theory

This section contains three papers, two of which argue that curriculum workers have not paid enough attention to the work of cognitive and developmental psychologists. William E. Doll builds primarily on the work of Piaget and Bruner. Doll maintains that competence can only be the result of the transformation of cognitive structures. He goes on to say that curriculum too often calls for student performance that embodies only a knowledge-copy view of learning.

Charles Letteri's paper stresses the importance of understanding learning styles in developing curriculum. However, unlike Doll, when Letteri discusses the nature of the curriculum process his assumptions are those of a control theorist.

David Williams' paper is not psychological in the same way that Doll's and Letteri's papers are. Williams attempts to warn curriculum workers of the dangers of accepting the prevailing psychological assumptions about the nature of people in relation to one another and to themselves. His paper cautions us that benevolent intentions in the absence of social consciousness are dangerous.

5. The Role of Contrast in the Development of Competence

William E. Doll, Jr.

The aim of instruction becomes the transformation of cognitive structure not just the mastery of a task.[1]

In this paper I will argue three propositions. First, that competence is different from performance in ways that make competency-based education quite different from performance-based education. Second, that historically the American schools have been, and continue to be, far more performance-oriented than competence-oriented. Third, that if a true competence model is to be developed then: (a) the existing knowledge-copy view of learning will have to be replaced by a knowledge-construct view, and (b) within this knowledge-construct view, *contrast*—in terms of alternatives, differences, dichotomies—*will play a major role*. The arguments used to support these propositions come from a variety of sources, but they are either compatible with, or based upon, the following assumption. As stated by Dewey that assumption reads—

. . . no thought, no idea, can possibly be conveyed as an idea from one person to another. When it is told, it is, to the one to whom it is told, another fact, not an idea. The communication may stimulate the other person to realize the question for himself and to think out a like idea, or it may smother his intellectual interest and suppress his dawning effort at thought. But *what he directly gets cannot be an idea. Only by wrestling with the conditions of the problem at first hand*, seeking and finding his own way out, *does he think*.[2]

[1] Nel Noddings. "Competence Theories and the Science of Education." *Educational Theory* 24 (4): 360; Fall 1974.

[2] John Dewey. *Democracy and Education*. New York: Free Press, 1916, 1966. pp. 159-60. (My emphasis.)

As stated by Piaget the assumption reads:

The problem of intelligence, and with it the central problem of the pedagogy of teaching, has thus emerged as linked with the fundamental epistemological problem of *the nature of knowledge; does the latter constitute a copy of reality or, on the contrary, an assimilation of reality into a structure of transformations?* . . . knowledge is derived from action, not in the sense of simple associative responses, but in the much deeper sense of the assimilation of reality into the necessary and general coordination of action. *To know an object is to act upon it and to transform it, in order to grasp the mechanisms of that transformation* as they function in connection with the transformative actions themselves. . . . it follows that intelligence, at all levels, is an assimilation of the datum into structures of transformation, and that these structurations consist in an organization of reality, whether in act or thought, and not in simply making a copy of it.[3]

These quotes are important because they form the heart of what Nel Noddings calls competence theorizing,[4] and what we at Oswego call developmentalism. Such theorizing assumes, as the quotes state, that the human mind has the (natural) ability to organize the data of the world via what Piaget calls schemata (structures of transformation), or what Bruner calls coding systems. It is the efficient and conscious development of these schemata that forms, for the developmentalist, the chief goal of schooling. As will be shown later, competence in this setting takes on quite a different set of meanings from those found in the literature on competency-based or performance-based education.

It is an irony that just after Chomsky had clearly and brilliantly separated performance from competence and explored the complex relation that exists between the two, educationists—apparently unaware of his work—have fused competence and performance. This fusion can be found throughout the literature. To cite but one example—

. . . a competency is a statement that describes the observable demonstration of a composite of the specific skills. The learning of a large list of individual skills is of little value unless these skills can be combined and interrelated so that, with practice, the result is a capability for a composite performance by the learner that is greater than the sum of the individual skills. A competency statement, then, is a description of those performances that are based on the acquisition, integration, composite building, and application of a set of related skills and knowledge.[5]

[3] Jean Piaget. *Science of Education and the Psychology of the Child*. New York: Grossman Publishers, 1971. pp. 28-29. (My emphasis.)

[4] Noddings, *op. cit.*

[5] Gene Hall and Howard Jones. *Competency-Based Education*. Englewood Cliffs, New Jersey: Prentice-Hall, Inc., 1976. pp. 29-30. Reprinted by permission of Prentice-Hall, Inc.

Here performance is clearly the main criterion of competency, with competence being defined, not in terms of itself but in terms of performance—specifically as a composition of individual performances. By enlarging the definition of performance to include competence the authors have: (a) ignored the qualitative distinction Chomsky has drawn between performance (as activity) and competence (as knowledge underlying activity), (b) ignored the etymological origins of the words (wherein performance refers to acts and competence refers to abilities), and (c) put forward, in another guise, the tenets of behavioral objectives.

Etymologically the word "performance" has referred to the doing or completing of an act. It grew out of the old French "parfournir" and was used as an antithesis to the concept of promises given but not completed. In the 15th, 16th, 17th centuries it was used to imply an act "carried through to completion," "accomplished entirely," "achieved." In more modern times the notion of "performance-as-doing" or "performance-as-finishing" has been revised to refer to the doing of a set routine in public view. Today the word essentially means "the formal execution of a definite act, or series of acts, done at an appointed time and place." Hence, when Artur Rubinstein gives a performance of Beethoven's 32nd Piano Sonata he is not merely "playing the piano"; rather, he is giving a formal recital, of a definite work, at an appointed time and place, before an appraising audience. How the audience appraises the performance—good or poor—cannot affect the question of whether it is or is not a performance; only whether it is or is not a good/poor performance. Performance itself is a value-neutral concept, and the quality of the act must be added to the act, since quality is not an integral part of the performance concept.

Historically the word "competence" is derived from the French "compétence," meaning a "fitness," a "sufficiency," an "aptitude," and from the Latin "competentia," meaning a "meeting together," an "agreement," a "symmetry," a "conjunction." In the English of the 16th and 17th centuries it came to be associated with possessing a "sufficiency of means," usually financial or personal, or "to adequately deal with a subject or situation." Today the word is used in this sense with the emphasis on the notion of ability to deal with, rather than on the dealing itself. It also carries with it the connotation of not possessing an excess of such abilities. In this sense competence is very much a value-laden word, stating as it does that the individual possesses sufficient but not excessive abilities. However (and this is key for the performance-competence distinction), the *possession* of abilities is not synonymous with the *use* of abilities. Hence, legal usage distinguishes between an individual's competence and his or her credibility. An individual may possess the powers to be credible, but still not be believed; analogously, an individual may possess powers of competence and still perform poorly. In point of fact, competence and performance although interrelated are qualitatively different: one referring to abilities, the other referring to acts.

The competence-performance relationship is a complex one. The young child saying "he goed" is both giving a poor performance and demonstrating competence. The performance is poor in that "goed" is grammatically incorrect; but at the same time "goed" is a demonstration of the child's knowledge of the structure of the past tense; taking the verb "go" and adding "ed." The grammatical incorrectness lies more in the irregularity of the verb tense than in the incompetence of the child. The same point can be made in regard to the adult native speaker's performance-competence patterns. An individual may perform well or poorly with language without giving an adequate sign as to how much he or she knows about the structural patterns of the language. Thus, Chomsky asserts, anyone using performance as the vehicle to assess competence must use performance in ways that are "devious and clever."

For Chomsky competence is knowledge of the rules of a given field, while performance is the way an individual utilizes these rules in a given situation. To quote Chomsky:

A person might memorize the performance table and perform on various simple-minded tests exactly as the performer who knows the rules of arithmetic, but this would not, of course, show that he knows these rules. It seems clear that the description which is of greatest psychological importance is the account of competence, not that of performance, both in the case of arithmetic and in the case of language. The deeper question concerns the kinds of structures the person has succeeded in mastering and internalizing, whether or not he utilizes them in practice, without interference from the many other factors that play a role in actual behavior. *For anyone concerned with intellectual processes*, or any question that goes beyond mere data arranging, *it is the question of competence that is fundamental. Obviously one can find out about competence only by studying performance, but this study must be carried out in devious and clever ways, if any serious result is to be obtained.*[6]

Obviously the schools in their educational processes have not adopted Chomsky's view, for instead of emphasizing competence they have emphasized performance, and instead of seeing the competence-performance relationship as complex they have seen it as simple—that is, those who perform well are competent, those who perform poorly are

[6] Noam Chomsky, "Formal Discussion" in a response to Miller and Ervin. "The Development of Grammar in Child Language." In: Ursula Bellugi and Roger Brown, editors. *The Acquisition of Language.* Chicago: University of Chicago Press, 1964, 1971. p. 36.

incompetent. The difficulty with this latter statement is more its simplistic approach to a complex issue than in its outright wrongness. The
results of this simplistic approach are dramatically seen in the way
schools have categorized, dealt with, and often failed certain minority
and immigrant groups. Here the work of Labov [7] with the language of
young blacks stands as a startling and continual reminder that competence cannot be assessed either directly or easily from performance. Less
dramatic but probably even more important is the fact that in assuming
competence to be merely an extension of performance, the schools
have not looked into competence to try to assess and develop "the kinds
of structures the person has succeeded in mastering and internalizing."
This assessment and development of internalized structures would be
the thrust of a genuinely competency-based educational program. In fact,
as the Chomsky quotes imply, it is hard to categorize a program with a
different thrust as truly educational.

Before moving on to define structure—the heart of the knowledge-
construct view—and the role contrast plays in the development of structures, it would be well to say a few words about the schools and the
performance-model they have adopted. As revisionist educational history
has shown, the social aspects of this performance-model have fitted in
quite well with America's commitment to industrialism. Since Frederick
Taylor first introduced his concept of engineering-efficiency to Bethlehem
Steel in the 1890's, America has adopted this model as a paradigm for
many, if not all, aspects of institutional organization. In adopting this
model the schools have merely reflected the dominant trend of American
social and industrial organization. Combined with this the schools have
adopted a model of learning based on a simplistic set of associationist
metaphors—for example, logically ordered presentations lead to better
understanding, repeated drill leads to successful performance, and successful performance produces competent individuals. These assumptions
have fitted in well with the industrial paradigm, and in some ways have
been extensions of it, for example, management by objectives as a learning theory. However, at a time when America was on both an expan-
sionist crusade and an industrial binge, when the number of school
children was doubling each decade, when the average classroom teacher
had hardly more than a contemporary eighth grade education, an industrial-performance model might have been all our society could reason-
ably expect or want in the schools. Such a model, though, will not meet
the requirements our society will place upon the schools in the future.

[7] William Labov. "The Logical Non-Standard English." In: F. Williams, editor.
Language and Poverty. Chicago: Markham Press, 1970.

As America moves further and further along the industrial continuum, into that area which Daniel Bell labels post-industrial, it will be less and less governed by simple notions of growth and efficiency, and more and more attention will be paid to advanced technology, sophisticated theory, social and personal concerns.

This triad will by no means form an easy or compatible partnership, for the change will require the schools (as institutions which have been delegated responsibility for both perpetuating and refining the culture) to come forth with a new educational model, one designed to meet the needs of a quite new society.[8] The present "back-to-basics" movement is not so much a wave of the future as it is, to borrow an analogy from Thomas Kuhn, a part of that final thrust to make the old paradigm work before it is replaced by the new. However, as Kuhn points out,[9] the new paradigm will have to include the advantages of the old along with solving the problems the old could not; and so, analogously, the new educational model—that which here is being labeled Developmentalism—will need to combine the better tenets of the behaviorist, industrial-performance model with the better tenets of the romanticist-humanist model. At a curriculum level this will mean the need to synthesize drill with open inquiry, the old math with the new, and phonics with linguistics. I believe the development of this model to be both a possibility and a necessity. Further, I believe the heart of the model to lie in the development of competence, as that term is being used here.

Competence, in this essay, refers to the possession and development of cognitive structures—structures that individuals use in organizing the world they perceive. A competent individual is one who has developed his/her mental structures to such an extent that he/she can deal with a problem and its tasks not only successfully but also creatively, heuristically, integratively. In other words a competent individual is indeed one who *can* perform well, but more than that, he/she is one who: (a) is conscious of his/her structurations, (b) has so developed these patterns that he/she can operate in a given field knowledgeably, imaginatively, efficiently. True competency-based education then would be designed to develop efficiently an individual's structural patternings. It is this that must form the primary aim of instruction. The conscious development of structure is not easy, however, for: (a) structures are not directly

[8] For the framework of the "post-industrial society" as Daniel Bell envisions it, see his *The Coming Post-Industrial Society*. New York: Basic Books, 1973, and *The Cultural Contradictions of Capitalism*. New York: Basic Books, 1976.

[9] Thomas Kuhn. *The Structure of Scientific Revolutions*. Chicago: University of Chicago Press, 1962, 1971. pp. 52-76.

observable (they must be inferred), (b) there is a fair amount of disagreement among those working in the field over ways to develop structures. Much of what is to follow must then be somewhat speculative and incomplete.

Essentially structures are organizational patterns; they are what the mind does with the material it perceives. They are the way the mind organizes reality. Piaget calls these structures "schema" and believes them to be hierarchically ordered with qualitative differences among the levels or stages of the hierarchy. Three of the main types of structure that Piaget has observed in children are the pre-operational, the concrete operational, and the formal operational. The qualitative differences among these three might best be illustrated by some examples.[10] When the child is operating in a pre-operational manner he/she will somewhat arbitrarily sort a graded series of ten sticks into some groups of two or three: something of the type such as small/large or small/medium/large combinations. The child operating with this structure will also need to measure sticks A and C to see which is longest when presented with the sticks in the form $A > B, B > C$. But when the child is operating in a concrete operational manner a totally different, a qualitatively different, structuration pattern appears. To quote Piaget, on the problem of ordering the ten sticks:

[Now] children go about seriation very systematically. They'll find the smallest stick and then place the smallest of all the sticks that remain next to it; then find the smallest of all the remaining ones and place it again until the whole series is constructed.[11]

When operating in this manner, or at this level, children will also begin to see that A "must be" longer than C, if $A > B$ and $B > C$. As Piaget says, they "experience *a feeling of necessity* apropos of transitive relationships."

They don't have to see the two sticks together; they just know that C must be shorter than A if A is larger than B and B is larger than C. This seems to verify to me the psychological existence of a structure even though structures as such are not observable. What we can observe, however, is a child's behavior in relation to things in his environment, and from this we can infer structure.[12]

Operating in a concrete operational structure is still somewhat confining, for, though the child can "experience a feeling of logical neces-

[10] Jean Piaget. "Some Aspects of Operations." In: Maria W. Piers, editor. *Play and Development*. New York: W. W. Norton, 1972. © 1972 by W. W. Norton & Co., Inc. pp. 17-22.

[11] *Ibid.*, p. 17.

[12] *Ibid.*, p. 18. (My emphasis.)

sity," the child is not yet able to articulate this "feeling" (the word "because" often being offered as sufficient justification as to why A > C), nor is the child able to generalize or transfer the feeling. When the child can operate in the formal operational manner he/she cannot only group the ten sticks serially and explain the transitive relationship between A and C, but he can also take the seriation action and the transitivity action and generalize upon them to develop the *concepts* of seriation and transitivity. It is this latter ability which Piaget prizes so much, and which he calls the logico-mathematical. It is also the quality which Piaget feels comprises the unique greatness of the human mind: the ability to get beyond the concrete to the abstract where the tremendous powers of logical reasoning reside.

While it is quite obvious from what has been presented that Piaget considers the structure of formal operations to be a norm or goal to attain, it is just as obvious that he has devoted little attention to analyzing the procedures one goes through in moving from one structuration pattern to another. In fact, Piaget dismisses such an emphasis as an "American one," and offers a number of experiments to show that it is generally futile to attempt a speed-up of the transition process. Yet Piaget is certainly no maturationist, only waiting for the transition to occur. Rather he calls himself an "interactionist," insisting that structures are actually created or constructed out of the interaction—particularly reflexive abstraction—taking place between an individual and the environment. To quote:

The truth is that I am neither a maturationist nor a neobehaviorist. I am an interactionist. What interests me is the creation of new thoughts that are not preformed, not predetermined by nervous system maturation nor predetermined by encounters with the environment, but are constructed within the individual himself, constructed internally through the process of reflexive abstraction and constructed externally through the process of experience.[13]

What one gets from such a quote, or what I get, is: (a) a sense of Dewey's statement that ideas are created, not given; (b) an awareness that ideas are truly new, at least to the individual, for they are his/her creations; (c) insight into the creation of ideas through the process of reflective abstraction built upon an active experience. All this leads me to hypothesize that for Piaget, the transition from one structure to another comes through the rich, full, active participation of the individual in that structure's quality—as Dewey uses the term "quality"—and where possible, notably in the more advanced ages of childhood, by having such participation include reflection on what one has done and why it was

13 *Ibid.*, p. 26.

done, as well as on what results it produced, and what directions might be taken in the future. From such a full, rich, experiential, and where possible reflective, participation in the quality of a given structure the possibilities, potentialities, and outlines of a new structure begin to emerge.

Bruner has in his espousal of the knowledge-construct view adopted a somewhat different and simpler view of structure than that of Piaget. Bruner does two things that Piaget does not do. First, he emphasizes the role external structures—particularly those of the disciplines—play in the development of internal structures; and second, he focuses quite heavily on the role contrast and conflict play in the intentional transition from one structure to another. Thus while Piaget will say that the teacher's task is to develop an experience richly and reflectively, Bruner will say:

The task of teaching a subject to a child at any particular age is one of representing the structure of that subject in terms of the child's way of viewing this.[14]

In this quote Bruner obviously accepts the Piagetian notion that children have characteristic ways of viewing the world, and he is quite willing to accept the corollary that children go through definite transformations in this structural process. However, he has an interest in teaching subjects that Piaget does not have, and a methodology for that teaching that Piaget at least questions. For Bruner the way to present a subject is to present the essential elements or structures of a subject in a (translated) form such that the learner can, fairly easily, assimilate these structures into an internal coding system. As an individual's own coding system becomes more developed (the structure more advanced) then more complex and sophisticated aspects of the subject can be presented. This developmental procedure is, of course, what Bruner calls the "spiral curriculum."

In regard to these internalized structures (or coding systems) themselves, Bruner sees them less as sequential hierarchies of the logico-mathematical and more as individual representation systems based on three modes: the enactive, the iconic, the symbolic. These modes appear in the child in the order listed, "each depending upon the previous one for its development." [15] Yet all remain intact throughout life, and the

[14] Jerome Bruner. "Readiness for Learning." In: J. Anglin, editor. *Beyond the Information Given.* New York: W. W. Norton, 1973. p. 413. Originally printed in: Jerome Bruner. *The Process of Education.* Cambridge, Massachusetts: Harvard University Press, 1960.

[15] Jerome Bruner, "The Course of Cognitive Growth." In: Anglin, *op. cit.*, p. 327. Much that I say about Bruner's thesis is drawn from this essay.

key to adult or mature ability is not so much the particular type of structure or representation mode the adult uses as it is the adult's ability to combine these modes into an "integrated sequence." To quote Bruner:

It is a truism that there are very few simple or single adult acts that cannot be performed by a young child. . . . *What higher skills require is that the component operatives be combined.* Maturation consists of an orchestration of these components into an integrated sequence.[16]

In Bruner's view it is this inability to combine representational modes that accounts for the child's failure in Piaget's classic conservation experiment: the child believes the tall, thin beaker has more water because it looks that way. In effect, the child is overwhelmed by the iconic mode of representation; if an object *looks larger* it must *be larger*. For Bruner the solution to this difficulty is to bring more than one mode of representation into play, and particularly to create a conflict between or among the modes of representation. Thus, he cites as meaningful to him, the results Françoise Frank achieved in attaining a conservation viewpoint with non-conserving children, ages 4 to 7, when she: (a) had them make a verbal commitment as to what would happen, and why, *before* she poured the water; (b) poured the water *behind a screen*; (c) removed the screen for all to "see." A short time later the usual form of the conservation experiment was run. The results were dramatic; compared either to a control group or to the original pretest, the Frank children going through the commitment, screening, seeing procedure performed 200 to 300 percent better.[17] It is intresting to note that this dramatic improvement applied only to the children age 5 and over; there was no observable effect on the 4-year-olds. From this and other experiments, Bruner concludes not only that "if the child is to succeed in the conservation task, he must have some internalized verbal formula that shields him from the overpowering appearance of the visual," but that in a larger sense,

We shall do better to conceive of growth as an empowering of the individual by multiple means for representing his world, multiple means that often conflict and create dilemmas that stimulate growth.[18]

This stimulus to growth leads, Bruner believes, to increased competence by helping the individual focus on and develop an internal struc-

16 *Ibid.* (My emphasis.) While Bruner is committed to the integration of the three modes of representation, he also believes the symbolic mode to possess the most imaginative and transforming powers.

17 *Ibid.*, pp. 335-38.

18 Jerome Bruner, "Representational Processes in Childhood." In: Anglin, *op cit.*, p. 323. (My emphasis.)

turation process or coding system. As such this concept of contrast is a particular elaboration of Dewey's notion of the role problems play in stimulating reflective thought, and of the role alternatives play in the development of that thought. While Piaget would in no way agree with Bruner that a conservation structure could be acquired easily or simply by creating a dilemma, he would readily accept the notion that contrast is a key ingredient in the knowledge-construct view of learning. That is, Piaget has offered evidence that the type of results Frank achieved were neither lasting nor generic—they could not be transferred to another task. On this basis Piaget considers Bruner's view on ways to achieve conservation or to move from one structuration to another as simplistic. Still Piaget emphasizes contrast himself when he says, as he frequently does, that "it is contact and above all contrast with the thoughts of others" that "causes a child to become conscious of himself." [19] This is to say, that as the child moves from an egocentric perspective to a socialized one, from a purely practical perspective to a logico-mathematical one, it is "conflict with the thought of others" that first shocks children into realizing that their own ways are not universal, and this leads them to the need for verification, which in turn opens up for them the symbolic and powerful world of the logico-mathematical. Thus, while Piaget rejects the particulars Bruner puts forth in regard to contrast, he accepts the general role contrast plays in the development of competence, especially in the progressive stages a child's thinking goes through as it moves from the egocentric and particular to the social and abstract.

At this point, I would like to suggest specific considerations for the teacher interested in developing competence in the classroom. For this I shall turn to Bruner, and particularly his essay "Going Beyond the Information Given." [20] I shall also focus on three considerations: (a) the "mind set" of the teacher, (b) the use of external structures, and (c) the role of contrast. One of the most noticeable differences between a competence-oriented and performance-oriented teacher is the evidence they look for. The following example taken from the workbook of a 6-year-old child illustrates this point. Along with other addition problems she had written:

$$2 + 2 + 2 = \not{6}$$
$$20 + 20 + 20 = 30$$
$$200 + 200 + 200 = 103$$

[19] Jean Piaget. *Judgment and Reasoning in the Child.* Totowa, New Jersey: Littlefield, Adams & Co., 1972. p. 25.

[20] Jerome Bruner, "Going Beyond the Information Given." In: Anglin, *op. cit.*, pp. 218-37, particularly 225-33.

The teacher had hoped the student would see the pattern of adding a zero for the tens and two zeros for the hundreds. While the child seems not to have grasped this, her performance is not devoid of competence. To one interested in probing the structurations this child used, the following hypothesis is worth further exploration: three tens equal thirty, three hundreds equal three hundred (written 103 due to a lack of experience), three units equal three (corrected to 6 because of much experience with 2 plus 2 plus 2). While it is impossible to tell without further questioning and observation of selected examples whether this hypothesis is correct, it is possible to assert that only a teacher interested in competence would bother to question what pattern, if any, underlay two wrong and one right answer. Thus, the competence-oriented teacher is one who will be looking beyond performance to assess competence, in terms of the structures used to arrive at a given solution or product. Such an orientation will take time and mean a rather major change in curricular proceedings. Probably fewer examples will be handled, but with more depth and analysis; more dialogue among students and between students and the teacher will probably occur; more selectivity and individualization of assignments will also probably occur. All this is based on the assumption that the competence-oriented teacher is continually searching for and trying to develop the patterns underlying performance; such a teacher will use answers not as finalities, but as introductions to the structurations of the learner.

While the foregoing was devoted to the development of internal structures, the second point will concern the use of external structures, that is, those structures which dominate and characterize a given field. It is Bruner's hypothesis that the teacher's craft consists in being able to so blend and intermix the individual's internal structures and the field's external structures that neither is subsumed by the other and both are developed. To do this he suggests, as do both Piaget and Dewey, that where possible an individual's structures or schemas be brought to consciousness and then compared with the structures others use, and particularly with the structures which dominate a given field. One way to do this is to have students compare ways of doing the same mathematics example, or compare reasons for interpreting the same piece of literature differently. Another way is to place drill work (certainly a necessary ingredient for competence) within a structured pattern. Thus, drill on multiplication facts could take the form of:

$$5 \times 5 = 25 \qquad 7 \times 7 = 49 \qquad 9 \times 9 = 81$$
$$4 \times 6 = 24 \qquad 6 \times 8 = 48 \qquad 8 \times 10 = 80$$

Here the student is not only receiving drill, but being introduced to and prepared for the more sophisticated algebraic concept that $n \times n = n^2$ while $(n - 1)(n + 1) = n^2 - 1$. From here it would be interesting to go on to the quantities $(n - 2)(n + 2)$ and $(n - 3)(n + 3)$ either algebraically or arithmetically. This sort of structuration, of course, is what Bruner refers to as the "spiral curriculum"—a curriculum where the student is introduced in a practical and intuitive way to that which later he will examine in an abstract and formal way.

The two foregoing considerations have dealt with the concept of structure; the first with the teacher searching for the individual's structures which have governed his or her activity, and the second with the teacher using the structures of the field to help the student better understand the field and his or her own structurations. The third consideration will deal with the role contrast plays in helping the student realize both structures. Bruner [21] and Olson [22] have done some beginning work in the use of contrast, and both conclude that *properly handled* contrast can lead the individual from the specific, nontransferable, short-term skills of performance to the generic, transferable, long-term skills of competence. The difficulty is that it is quite easy to mishandle contrast. At the adult level there is a definite tendency to reject, ignore, or assimilate contrast so that it loses its effect. Thus, it is necessary to present contrast in a framework whereby it becomes anomalous, that is, where it almost but doesn't quite fit into existing schemes. In this way it becomes bothersome, annoying, noticeable, and potentially resolvable. All of these are necessary. At the junior level children are still forming schemas and quickly become confused when much conflicting or contrary information is presented to them. Thus Bruner hypothesizes that in dealing with contrast one needs to give the individual a lot of drill on those factors which will be placed (consciously) within a pattern, and the development of patterns must be done in such a way that the individual is encouraged to be "combinatorially playful" without the fear of performance failure. This use of drill and combinatorial playfulness is designed to encourage the learner to experiment, but to experiment with components he/she understands well and feels comfortable with. It is this unique combination which is necessary if contrast is to fulfill its function of developing competence. To quote Bruner:

[21] Jerome Bruner, "The Role of Overlearning and Drive Level in Reversal Learning," *op. cit.*, pp. 186-97; and "The Perception of Incongruity: A Paradigm." In: Anglin, *op. cit.*, pp. 68-82.

[22] David Olson. *Cognitive Development: The Child's Acquisition of Diagonality.* New York: Academic Press, 1970.

It would seem, then, that *under conditions of high drive*, if *a path* to the goal has been learned, it is learned, so to speak, as this path to this goal and *is not coded or acquired as an example of a more generic pattern.*

(Obviously Bruner is objecting to the performance, high drive, strong motivation model so evident in schools today.)

In sum, then, the question of mastery comes down to this. Learning often cannot be translated into a generic form until there has been enough mastery of the specifics of the situation to permit the discovery of lower-order regularity.

(Please refer back to the example of the six-year-old child on page 60. It was mastery of the specifics which allowed her to see her mistake in line one, but not in line three.)

Unless one is exposed to some changes, genericizing does not seem to be stimulated . . . for only in the face of changes in events does one begin to have the information necessary to abstract generic properties.[23]

The development of competence is definitely one of abstracting generic properties from the material studied. It depends upon the skillful integration of internal and external structures, and the adroit use of contrast to make those structures evident. It is very demanding upon the teacher in terms of time and intellect. However, the rewards are great; for a competence model offers to the teacher the opportunity to participate with students in the development of types of growth, meaning, and insight that a performance model can never achieve. And, ironically, a well-developed competence model can ultimately offer better performance than even the best developed performance model.

[23] Jerome Bruner, "Going Beyond the Information Given." In: Anglin, *op. cit.*, pp. 228, 232, 233. (My emphasis, my comments.)

6. Cognitive Style: Implications for Curriculum

Charles A. Letteri

The demand and right of an individual to equal educational opportunity have had only a partial response from the education community in general and from curriculum designers in particular. To place children, by whatever means, in the presence of somewhat equal educational elements such as materials, facilities, and personnel does not ensure they have equal access to those elements. By equal access, I mean possession of a repertoire of intellectual or cognitive processes and abilities necessary to effectively and efficiently learn from an educational environment. These processes and abilities, defined here as Cognitive Styles, are prerequisite to learning itself and must become the foundation for the design of future curriculum.

Therefore in order to address the issue of equal access, the designers of curriculum must first establish a sound theoretical base vis-à-vis basic cognitive processes and abilities (cognitive styles).[1] In addition, curriculum designers must ensure that each individual learner is taught and can effectively utilize them in a learning situation. The various dimensions of cognitive style constitute the unique modes of intellectual operation that an individual employs when attempting to learn. Stated simply, cognitive styles are how an individual learns and "how to learn is in itself something that has to be learned, though it is rarely taught

---

[1] V. G. Labouvie, J. R. Liwin, and K. A. Urberg. "The Relationship Between Cognitive Abilities and Learning—A Second Look." *Journal of Educational Research* 67 (4): 558-69; 1975.

in the schools." [2] The purpose of this paper is to explore the implications of cognitive style research for curriculum design.

"Cognitive styles are information processing habits. They are characteristic modes of operation which, although not necessarily completely independent of content, tend to function across a variety of content areas." [3] They "are ways of achieving intellectual goals which are general enough to be characteristic of a large segment of one individual's activity and to distinguish that individual from other individuals in search of the same goals. Their stability suggests that considerable use can be made of these concepts in the description and explanation of human behavior." [4]

Researchers have been able to identify several such styles or continuums: Field Dependence-Independence; Scanning; Breadth of Categorizing; Conceptualizing Styles; Cognitive Complexity-Simplicity; Reflectiveness-Impulsivity; Leveling-Sharpening; Constricted-Flexible Control; Tolerance for Incongruity.[5]

These cognitive dimensions would appear to be the basis for *how* an individual perceives stimulus situations and items, and therefore determine *what* the individual perceives. In turn these dimensions would indicate *how* the individual processes the information thus perceived and therefore determines *what* the individual learns (knowledge, skills, values). As a result, the individual's reactions, behavior, and performance would partially be predicated on that knowledge base.

Recent studies have found significant relationships between cognitive style and certain intellectual tasks, such as: reading English prose; math and physical sciences; geography, serial learning; general problem solving; concept identification; certain school subjects; reading,[6] as well as significant correlations between cognitive style and concept learning

[2] D. C. Jordan. "ANISA*: A New Comprehensive Early Education Model for Developing Human Potential." *Journal of Research and Development in Education* 6 (3): 83-93; Spring 1973.

[3] S. Messick. "The Criterion Problem in the Evaluation of Instruction: Assessing Possible, Not Just Intended, Outcomes." In: Len Sperry, editor. *Learning Performance and Individual Differences.* Glenview, Illinois: Scott, Foresman, 1972.

[4] L. E. Bourne, B. R. Ekstrand, and R. L. Dominowski. *The Psychology of Thinking.* Englewood Cliffs, New Jersey: Prentice-Hall, Inc., 1971. p. 234.

[5] *Ibid.*

[6] See, for example: C. R. Brooks and T. N. Clair. "Relationship Among Visual Figure Ground Perceptions, Word Recognition, I.Q., and Chronological Age." *Perception and Motor Skills* 36; 1976; D. J. Scatterly. "Cognitive Style, Spatial Ability, and School Achievement." *Journal of Educational Psychology* 68 (1): 36-42; 1976; P. M. Sunshine and F. Di Vesta. "Effects of Density and Format on Letter Discrimination by Beginning Readers with Different Learning Styles." *Journal of Educational Psychology* 68 (1): 15-19; 1976.

abilities.[7] The trend in these findings is clear, a significant relationship does exist between a child's cognitive style and his/her ability to learn and perform in school. This leads us to the basic hypothesis of this paper: *An individual's cognitive style is a basic intellectual determinant in his/her level of achievement or success in educational environments.*

Current research in cognitive styles, in the main, seeks correlations between an individual's extreme position on a specific cognitive style continuum (e.g., Field Dependence-Independence) and his/her personality traits (for example, articulated life goal, self-concept); *or* intellectual tasks (subtests of Weschler, mathematics performance).

The issue I am raising is that two or more of the cognitive style continuums may be involved in any one intellectual task performance. Therefore, to seek only dichotomous correlations may not provide the investigator with a complete picture of the entire cognizing event.

In contrast, I am concerned with an individual's cognitive *profile* as opposed to his/her positioning on only one of the cognitive style continuums. By cognitive profile I am referring to the position of an individual across all nine previously mentioned cognitive style continuums on a diagram. This profile makes it possible to study the interrelationships between the continuums of cognitive style and their combined impact on performance levels in a given learning task. For example, by constructing cognitive profiles it would be possible to determine which profile(s) relates to high performance and which profile(s) relates to low performance. Further it might be possible to determine if a particular cognitive profile is the appropriate one needed by most individuals to be successful in a specific learning task.

The reverse is also possible, that is, we could analyze a specific learning task and determine what would be the appropriate cognitive profile before presenting the task to learners. In this way learners who do not possess the appropriate cognitive profile could receive training to modify their inappropriate cognitive profiles.

I am currently testing subjects across seven dimensions of cognitive style (Category Width; Cognitive Complexity-Simplicity; Scanning; Leveling-Sharpening; Reflective-Impulsive; Field Dependent-Independent; and Tolerance for Incongruity). For eighth grade students, two articulated and opposite profiles have emerged. One profile describes high academic performers and the other profile describes low academic performers, as measured by standardized achievement tests, grade point averages, and I.Q. The next phase of the research will involve modifying

[7] A. J. Davis. "Cognitive Style: Methodological and Developmental Consideration." *Child Development* 42: 1447-59; 1971.

low performers' cognitive profiles to be similar to that of high performers and determine the impact of modified profiles on performance level changes.

By describing cognitive style in terms of a profile we can also ask questions not otherwise possible. For example, is it possible for a cognitively simple, field dependent, broad categorizing individual to attain the highest levels of Kohlberg's moral development stages, or achieve and perform at the formal operations level of hypo-thetico deductive reasoning, or reach the self actualization stage of Maslow's hierarchy of needs? Could such an individual cognize symbolic data (Bruner) or reorganize a stimulus pattern in a problem solving situation (gestalt) or discriminate along specific dimensions of a stimulus needed in discrimination or paired associates learning? Is the ability to perform transductive reasoning (Piaget, pre-operational) dependent on a more primitive/antecedent cognitive skill such as being able to distinguish a portion of a stimulus from its total configuration (field dependent-independent) as well as being able to retain that discrimination distinctly in long term memory (leveling-sharpening) so as to serve as a standard? These questions point out that the types of learning or developmental tasks presented to individuals may require, for success, prerequisite and basic cognitive processes and abilities, that is, an appropriate cognitive profile. But the development of the style (strategies) or level of cognitive functioning needed for differing situations cannot be solely accounted for through either developmental stages (Piaget) or relationships established between a given situation (moral stage) and development.

Flavell raises this issue, albeit in a different context, "Piaget argues that all significant cognitive development advances are made through equilibration. There appear to be problems with Piaget's equilibration model. In order for equilibration to take place the child would seem to need the ability or disposition to do four things in sequence. "Since a given child could lack one or more of these four prerequisites in relation to some specific cognitive problem, it is obvious that he may not be able to complete or even begin a Piagetian process of equilibration with respect to it"; and further, "Different sets of processes may typically be involved in different kinds of cognitive acquisition. Different individuals may even use different processes to acquire the same things." [8]

Much of the recent literature and research has demonstrated that either directed training or modeling is effective in changing the cognitive style (and strategies) of the individual learner with a corresponding

[8] H. Flavell. *Cognitive Development.* Englewood Cliffs, New Jersey: Prentice-Hall, Inc., 1977. pp. 241-43.

change in his/her performance in learning tasks.[9] Yet, schools do not concentrate on teaching those basic skills and strategies. Curriculum itself does not develop the how of learning, or provide the training necessary for success in school. As Jordan [10] stated, "How to learn is in itself something that has to be learned, though it is rarely taught in the schools."

We have a sound research base for "learning how to learn" theory, with direct instructional and evaluation implications as well as articulated teaching strategies. I am proposing, therefore, a new basis for the establishment of educational goals and for curriculum design and evaluation. Our efforts should be directed toward the development of curriculum procedures, based on the analysis of learning tasks, to establish the prerequisite cognitive profile needed for achievement and success. We could then directly intervene and modify—through training—an individual's inappropriate cognitive profile in order for the learner to have the power to be self-directive and successful in terms of his or her learning. The result would be moving one step closer to ensuring equal access to learning from educational environments in addition to the equal opportunity of being in their presence.

Until we address this cognitive profile question, we will have negated or ignored a most important issue in teaching/learning situations. Unless children and adults are instructed, trained, in the cognitive profile for specific learning tasks, the learner is the victim of trial and error; and success in educational situations is left merely to chance.

Curriculum therefore must take cognizance of an individual's cognitive profile in terms of materials and presentation, while intervening to modify a child's or an adult's cognitive profile so as to facilitate the acquisition of a cognitive repertoire that can be successfully applied in a self-directed mode across a host of learning problems and situations. Curriculum research, in the future, therefore, should be directed not merely to the question of what is appropriate for a person's developmental level in terms of content and materials, but more important to the questions of:

[9] See, for example: B. B. Barrat. "Training and Transfer in Combinatorial Problem Solving: The Development of Formal Reasoning During Early Adolescence." *Developmental Psychology* 11: 700-704; 1975; D. R. Denny. "Modeling Effects Upon Conceptual Style and Cognitive Tempo." *Child Development* 47: 105-10; 1972; E. R. Heider. "Information Processing and the Modification of an Impulsive Conceptual Tempo." *Child Development* 42: 1276-81; 1971; A. M. Howie. "Effects of Brief Exposure to Symbolic Model Behavior on the Information Processing Strategies of Internally and Externally Oriented Children." *Developmental Psychology* 11 (3): 325-33.

[10] Jordan, *op. cit.*

1. What is an appropriate cognitive profile for specific learning tasks?

2. How can an individual's acquisition of an appropriate cognitive profile for success in specific learning situations be facilitated and evaluated?

3. How can these data and this information be incorporated into the curriculum for each prospective teacher at teacher training institutions?

4. How can the acceptance of cognitive profile as a denominator for all children, as well as serving as the statement relative to their success and achievement in academic situations, be facilitated?

5. How can we ensure that all children are involved in a "learning how to learn" environment regardless of the physical or emotional state of their being?

6. How can we ensure that all children have equal access to as well as opportunity to benefit from similar learning environments?

7. The Therapeutic Curriculum

David C. Williams

In a recent *Time* magazine survey, several psychiatrists claimed that nearly half of their clients suffered principally from narcissism. Writing in *The Christian Science Monitor*, Melvin Maddocks similarly observed the "spiritual supermarket" in what has become, in Tom Wolfe's term, "The Age of Me." The popular literature market bulges with "how to" manuals on gaining and keeping power, pinpointing psycho-corporeal "hot spots," securing "creative" divorces and marriages, "making it" with other persons, and perfecting skills in getting made. For the affluent, there are sex surrogates, biofeedback gadgetry, cocaine, and a cornucopia of massage and meditation styles. For everyone else, as tradition would have it, there is a mass education response with prosaic "coping skill" and "proficiency" training. There is, of course, considerable precedence for therapeutic curriculum events.

For over a decade, schooling has blended with pharmacology to promote Ritalin in thousands of schools. Likewise, behavioral therapeutics is evident in performance contracting strategies employing "token economy" controls. For curriculum, the problem is the emergence of educational program planning as the delivery system for the worldview of the therapeutic.[1] Resurrection of earlier 20th century emphases on overtness and observability in curriculum goals is one element of this process. Another centers on the field's gradual adoption of the control language by the "helping" professions.

[1] More detailed analysis of the therapeutic curriculum may be requested from the author.

The curriculum field is confronted with this problem for at least two reasons. One is global, involving the increased dependence of the newer human service professions on modern psychology and its ideologies. This has wrought a decline in attention to spiritual, political, and social dimensions, as Philip Rieff and others have noted in the post-Freudian demise of faith. A second reason for a problem is curriculum's continued dependence on public schools as a universal model and testing ground. The field has thus neglected important non-school learning systems, and has been caught in the bind of public education's proclivity for accepting responsibility for everything. The dominant feeling seems to be that if curriculum cannot muster adequate resources in combatting *all* the afflictions of the overeducated as well as the undereducated, it should command at least the appearances of being able to do so. Hence, the banal reliance on competencies, proficiencies, performance criteria, contracting, and near-deification of immediate observability as a curriculum standard.

There is certainly some basis, however, for castigating "vague, high-sounding hopes and aspirations," as Bobbitt called them, when they have been passed off as curriculum goals. Current fervor for explicit performance criteria differs very little from his proposals for "scientific" determination of curriculum goals. One may recall that, for Dewey, science entailed reliance on reflective inquiry into the real daily problems of living, and then acting on discovery through civic action. For Bobbitt, however, science was ossified by stolid regard for logical-positivist forms of justification and the presumption of static social enterprises. The danger in enthusiam for this mode, noted later by Boyd Bode, is "that it obscures the need for breaking from old standards and old ideals." Schools with curricula so founded obstruct "changes leading to a more democratic form of social organization." In developing curriculum goals, one might ultimately find that the "refinement of technique is no substitute for insight."

The rise of therapy and the curriculum share many qualities. Most significant among these is disdain for theory, frequently observed as a shortcoming in psychoanalysis as well as education. The curriculum mindset that theory is largely inappropriate to the field has left it adrift in a sea of ideas swollen with mechanistic behavioral assumptions. The field has merely followed the path of least resistance. This has also become the path to greater funding, as federal and state agencies seek to become more "accountable," which is only the most recent among several euphemisms for "auditable." Another powerful force in curriculum is a deterministic presumptiveness best described by Ronald Laing's image that "seen as an organism, man cannot be anything but a complex of things, of *its,* and the processes that ultimately comprise an organism are *it*-processes."

Personal as well as program planning have come under the influence of behavioral therapeutics. Liam Hudson has argued that beliefs that "people are bodies, and bodies are things" have been instilled through "psychic engineering." This process has undertaken the alteration of human awareness while promulgating doctrines that "physical events are 'real,' while mental ones are not." In everyday life, a consequence of this doctrine has been a sort of objective narcissism. A contemporary *leitmotif* is extreme self-absorption in psychic and psycho-physical gratification. As Christopher Lasch has suggested, "a growing despair of changing society—even of understanding it—has generated on the one hand a revival of old-time religion, and on the other a cult of expanded consciousness, health, and personal 'growth.'" In this social setting, political and theoretical questions about curriculum must be addressed. Why has educational program planning so complacently labored under the influence of behavioristic therapeutics? What are the alternatives?

Part IV

Classroom Practice and Curriculum Theory

In their paper Walter Doyle and Gerald Ponder discuss how the success or failure of educational innovations is largely determined by teachers' perceptions of what is practical. Their discussion of the dimensions of why a particular innovation is or is not likely to be considered practical makes it clear that practical is defined by the pattern of existing relationships within the school. Doyle and Ponder argue for what they call an ecological approach to curriculum innovation.

Bernice Wolfson's paper calls attention to the importance and power of the beliefs of the teacher in any classroom transaction. She identifies six critical assumptions that make up the teaching-learning situation and then shares her perceptions of each assumption. Curriculum, according to Wolfson, is what teachers and students together create. It is not something that others develop and force upon the teacher and the students. She seems to be suggesting that a basic issue in education is the nature and quality of the human interaction that exists in schools.

8. The Ethic of Practicality: Implications for Curriculum Development

Walter Doyle and Gerald Ponder

Any curriculum proposal, regardless of its merits, will have little impact on schooling until it is used. But the weight of experience suggests strongly that it has been far easier to propose new curricula or ways to implement new proposals than it has to *accomplish* curriculum implementation. In an attempt to come to grips with this rather consistent failure to change curriculum practice, analysts have recently focused on processes that occur during implementation. In studies of these processes it has become increasingly clear that the teacher, as user of curriculum, plays a key role in the fate of any implementation program.[1]

The present analysis focuses on ways of thinking about the classroom teacher as user of curriculum and the ways teachers react to curriculum proposals. The analysis is based on the premise that characteristics of a curriculum have *meanings* for teachers and that these meanings determine in significant ways the adoption and use of a curriculum proposal.[2] A common and continuing problem in implementation is the discrepancy between what a curriculum proposal means to its designers and what it means to teachers who are being asked to use it. Assump-

[1] See: M. Fullan. "Overview of the Innovative Process and the User." *Interchange* 3 (2-3): 1-46; 1972; and G. Hall. "The Study of Individual Teacher and Professor Concerns About Innovations." *Journal of Teacher Education* 27 (1): 22-23; 1976.

[2] C. Geertz. *The Interpretation of Cultures.* New York: Basic Books, 1973; P. L. Berger and T. Luckmann. *The Social Construction of Reality.* Garden City, New York: Doubleday, 1967.

tions about the origins and nature of this discrepancy would seem to underlie any model designed to increase the probability of success in implementing—and subsequently evaluating—curriculum proposals, and it is the nature of these underlying assumptions that must be elaborated before proceeding with a discussion of the elements of the ethic of practicality.

Images of the Teacher as Curriculum User

In the literature on curriculum implementation, thinking about the teacher tends to be conducted in terms of one of two general images: the teacher as "rational adopter" or the teacher as "stone-age obstruction-ist."[3] A brief review of these common images will underscore the distinctive characteristics of the approach to thinking about the teacher as curriculum user delineated in this paper. Implementation is most often approached as a highly systematic, rational process. These imple-mentation models emphasize intellectual processes such as problem identification, data search, and assessment—processes which *should* determine the course of implementation. Strategies in this model, in other words, stress information dissemination and deliberative mecha-nisms as key mediators of change. Not surprisingly, teachers do not always behave "rationally." To some change strategists, in fact, teachers act as "stone-age obstructionists," resisters to change who defend the status quo with folklore and rationalization. From this perspective, the strategist's task is to bypass the teacher by installing a "teacher-proof" curriculum.

Rational or not, teachers are impossible to bypass. Despite highly formalized and heavily structured plans, teachers *adapt,* rather than adopt, curriculum proposals. They are in fact the ultimate arbiters of classroom practice. And, in arbitrations of classroom practice, they appear to employ what might best be called an *ethic of practicality.* The essential features of this ethic can be summarized briefly as follows. Careful listening to the way teachers talk about recommendations for classroom practice soon makes it clear that the concept "practical" is used frequently and consistently to label such statements. In the context of the present analysis, this label represents a central ingredient in the meaning teachers assign to a proposed change in classroom procedure. It is, in other words, a nontechnical expression of the "taken-for-granted

[3] The discussion of teacher images is based on: S. D. Sieber. "Images of the Practitioner and Strategies of Educational Change." *Sociology of Education* 45: 362-85; 1972.

world" of the practitioner.[4] Recommendations seen as "practical" will be incorporated, at least tentatively, into teacher plans. Those perceived as impractical have little chance of being tried unless control mechanisms, such as those that frequently accompany innovation projects, make teacher decision making superfluous. The study of the practicality ethic, then, is the study of the meaning curriculum proposals have for teachers and the way in which these meanings determine the extent to which teachers will attempt to modify classroom practices.[5]

The Ethic of Practicality

The major question for the present analysis is: What determines practicality? In other words, what attributes of a change proposal tend to elicit the perception of practicality from teachers? This question cannot be answered here with any empirical adequacy since the issue itself has seldom been formulated in this manner. It is possible, however, to conceptualize several possible dimensions of the practicality ethic on the basis of existing evidence. Such a procedure should be especially useful in stimulating further research on what appears to be a key element in the innovation process.

The rational adopter image of the teacher carries with it the implica-

[4] The conceptual significance of the "taken-for-granted world" of the practitioner is delineated in: A. Schutz. *Collected Papers.* Volumes 1 and 2. The Hague: Martinus Nijhoff, 1962-1964; and H. Garfinkel. "Remarks on Ethnomethodology." In: J. J. Gumperz and D. Hymes, editors. *Directions in Sociolinguistics: The Ethnography of Communication.* New York: Holt, Rinehart, and Winston, 1972.

[5] A word about the origins of the practicality ethic will help context the present discussion. The authors maintain that teachers' emphasis on practicality is a natural result of experience with the demands imposed by the distinctive ecology of the classroom. Teachers are the final arbiters of classroom practice, for example, because of the normal conditions of relative isolation from adult surveillance and the resulting functional autonomy under which they work. Further, the demands engendered by the task of managing relatively large groups of nonvolunteer students over fairly long periods of time lead teachers to be vitally concerned with the possible immediate consequences of disrupting established practice. From the ecological vantage point, it would seem reasonable that teachers might react to change proposals more as "pragmatic skeptics" than as "rational adopters" or "stone-age obstructionists." For a major basis of the ecological perspective, see: R. Barker. *Ecological Psychology.* Stanford, California: Stanford University Press, 1968. The concept of classroom ecology is elaborated in greater detail in: W. Doyle and G. Ponder. "Classroom Ecology: Some Concerns About a Neglected Dimension of Research on Teaching." *Contemporary Education* 46: 183-88; 1975; W. Doyle. "The Uses of Nonverbal Behaviors: Toward an Ecological Model of Classrooms." *Merrill-Palmer Quarterly* 23 (3); 1977; and W. Doyle. "Paradigms for Research on Teacher Effectiveness." In: L. S. Shulman, editor. *Review of Research in Education.* Volume 5. Itasca, Illinois: F. E. Peacock, 1977.

tion that a practical proposal is one in which the weight of evidence favoring a particular proposal should be a sufficient condition for its adoption. A less simplistic and more realistic position is that decisions about practicality result from the complex interaction of several varia- bles. In this initial attempt to conceptualize the practicality ethic, we have posited that teachers appear to use three general criteria to deter- mine if a statement about classroom procedures qualifies as "practical." We have designated these criteria *instrumentality, congruence,* and *cost.* Despite some overlap, these dimensions seem to represent distinct aspects of meaning associated with the ethic of practicality. In essence, these dimensions define the "rules" for applying the term to actual change proposals.

Instrumentality. To qualify minimally as practical, a proposal must contain instrumental content. That is, a change proposal must describe an innovation procedure in terms which depict classroom contingencies. This suggests that instrumental content—communicating the innovation in procedural, ecologically relevant terminology—is a necessary condi- tion for eliciting initial teacher evaluation of the practical merit of a change proposal. Statements of principle or specifications of desired out- comes are not "practical" largely because they lack the necessary proce- dural referents.

The instrumentality dimension is particularly significant for two reasons. First, teachers often complain that innovations are seldom com- municated clearly. This lack of clarity appears to be directly related to the absence of procedural content. Without this degree of understanding communicated by procedural specifications, teacher judgment concerning the practicality of a change proposal is nearly impossible. Second, con- verting principles and outcome specifications into appropriate procedures is a demanding task, a task that most classroom teachers have neither the skills nor the time to accomplish.

Evidence related to the communication of innovations and the task of conversion from principles to procedures strongly suggests that *enactment in the setting* is a major factor in interpreting the instrumen- tality of a change proposal. In their review of adoption and implementa- tion of innovations, for example, Berman and McLaughlin found that teachers strongly preferred concrete "how-to-do-it" workshops on in- novation procedures rather than inspirational or theoretical sessions on the rationale for or projected outcomes of the innovation.[6] This report

[6] P. Berman and M. W. McLaughlin. "Implementation of Educational Innovation." *The Educational Forum* 60: 345-70; 1976.

also suggested that having teachers develop their own project materials rather than adopting pre-packaged materials can be crucial to the successful implementation of the project. As Berman and McLaughlin expressed it, "The exercise of 'reinventing the wheel' can provide an important opportunity for staff to work through and understand project precepts and to develop a sense of 'ownership' in project methods and goals." [7]

Congruence. Instrumentality alone, however, does not determine practicality. Teachers also make decisions in terms of the extent to which a proposed procedure is congruent with perceptions of their own situations. Evidence for this congruence dimension is contained, for example, in the frequently-expressed concern teachers have for the way their students will react to an innovation.[8] At this writing, congruence appears to be comprised of a cluster of elements all focusing on the perceived "match" between the change proposal and prevailing conditions. The emphasis throughout is personal. One teacher in the Dienes and Connelly case study expressed this personal dimension of congruence in the statement:

I can't believe that there is a machine that could be programmed in all the complexity necessary to teaching some of the concepts which I am teaching. . . .[9]

At a minimum, there appear to be three aspects of congruence. The first relates to the proposal itself: Does the procedure fit the way the teacher normally conducts classroom activities? Practices which depart radically from normal conditions are usually viewed as impractical, often on the grounds of possible adverse student reaction. The second aspect of congruence involves perceptions of the origins of the proposal and, in many cases, the spokesperson for the innovation. Teachers respond, in other words, to the nature of the setting under which the procedure was tried previously and to the experiential credentials of the person making the recommendation. A practice, for example, which is known to work in an upper-middle-class suburban high school may often be per-

[7] *Ibid.*, p. 361.

[8] A. Tom. "Teacher Reaction to a Systematic Approach to Curriculum Implementation." *Curriculum Theory Network* 11; Spring 1973; P. W. Jackson and E. Belford. "Educational Objectives and the Joys of Teaching." *School Review* 73; Autumn 1965; D. C. Lortie. "The Balance of Control and Autonomy in Elementary School Teaching." In: A. Etzioni, editor. *The Semi-Professions and Their Organization.* New York: Free Press, 1969.

[9] B. Dienes and F. M. Connelly. "A Case Study of Teacher Choice and Deliberation." Paper presented at the Annual Meeting of the American Educational Research Association, New Orleans, 1973. p. 5.

ceived as impractical by teachers in an inner-city school, especially when communicated by a university consultant. Finally, teachers appear to judge procedures in terms of their compatibility with self-image and preferred mode of relating to students. This dimension of congruence is especially evident in teacher reactions to behavior modification procedures. Although a teacher may be convinced that such procedures "work," he or she may feel that the role of contingency manager does violence to the student-teacher relationship.

It is clear from these brief comments that congruence serves a conserving function in maintaining conventional classroom procedures. Such a conclusion is consistent, at least, with the prevailing evidence that most "changes" in school practice involve little more than a rearrangement of existing patterns and processes.[10] The existence of a conserving attitude among teachers is understandable in view of the fact that they bear the immediate brunt of any failure to maintain a functional school program.

Cost. The final criterion of practicality is best described by the term "cost." In our usage, cost may be conceptualized as a ratio between amount of return and amount of investment. It refers primarily to the ease with which a procedure can be implemented and the potential return for adopting an innovation. The extent to which a proposed practice can be broken down into smaller units for short-term trials, for example, obviously reduces the cost of innovating. Since many educational innovations involve major structural reorganizations, cost is usually high. A great deal of effort must be invested to achieve an unknown amount of return. Data to support the role of the cost dimension are contained in Stephens' study.[11] He found that teachers would adopt innovations, even despite moderate personal skepticism, if the reward structure of the school was made contingent upon innovativeness. It is important to note that the notions of cost and reward used here are not solely matters of monetary remuneration. Teachers are especially responsive to social factors, such as recognition and student enthusiasm. Since costs appear to rise as an implementation program progresses, the cost factor would seem to play an important role in the gradual decline which tends to characterize the latter stages of innovation projects.[12]

[10] D. Orlosky and B. O. Smith. "Educational Change: Its Origins and Characteristics." *Phi Delta Kappan* 53; March 1972. See, also: E. R. House. *The Politics of Educational Innovation.* Berkeley, California: McCutchan, 1974.

[11] T. Stephens. "Innovative Teaching Practices: Their Relation to System Norms and Rewards." *Educational Administration Quarterly* 10; Winter 1974.

[12] N. Gross, J. B. Giacquinta, and M. Bernstein. *Implementing Organizational Innovations.* New York: Basic Books. 1971.

Conclusion

To review, the major theme of this paper has been that curriculum implementation is determined in large measure by teacher reaction to change proposals and by the ways teachers use innovations in the classroom. Further, it is our contention that user reaction to curriculum proposals derives from the distinctive ecology of the classroom and the set of demands on teachers that arises from that ecological system. Given that context, it is not surprising that curriculum proposals based almost entirely on learner outcomes to the exclusion of normal classroom contingencies face great implementation difficulties. Further, given the wide variation in types of schools and classrooms, it would seem that federal and local policies that attempt to maximize the dissemination of innovation projects would achieve a low rate of success in transferring projects to dissimilar settings. From the standpoint of curriculum effectiveness, policies stressing localization, or development and implementation within a specific setting such as a single school or similar classrooms within a school, would seem to have a greater chance of impacting practice because of the heightened ecological validity resulting from the increased attention to context variables.

In like manner, curriculum evaluation and curriculum research could be strengthened by greater attention to the contexts in which curriculum practice occurs. Curriculum evaluation designs especially tend to be "context-free" through lack of consideration of the ecology of the classroom. In their current reliance on antecedent and outcome measures, evaluation designs treat classroom practices largely as variables to be measured in terms of discrepancies between intentions and actions. Teacher practices thus tend to be treated as "intangibles" or "uncontrollables" rather than as regularities to be studied and analyzed. In sum, it would seem that a different perspective—one that views teacher practices during the implementation process as naturally occurring phenomena to be analyzed rather than as impediments to be controlled or bypassed—holds promise for research on and evaluation of curriculum innovations. Such perspective may eventually offer useful interpretive tools for understanding how teachers make decisions and how to construct materials and procedures that will have greater potential for changing classroom practice.

9. A Phenomenological Perspective on Curriculum and Learning

Bernice J. Wolfson

As you know, titles for presentations are determined long before the ideas are assembled and the meanings developed. As I began to reflect on the meaning of this title, I became aware that I would be talking about *my* phenomenological perspective, not "a" phenomenological perspective. Indeed, I could hardly do otherwise!

It is my assumption that each human-being-in-the-world speaks from a unique perspective reflecting a particular history, a private construction of the world, and a personal set of beliefs and values. We also speak in a particular context and at a certain point in time, both of which are, of course, transient.

You will recognize in this assumption the residue of ideas which have permeated our intellectual life from the thinking of those philosophers and psychologists who are variously called, phenomenologists, humanists, perceptual psychologists, existentialists, or poets. Emily Dickinson [1] expressed this assumption when she said:

> Without the snow's tableau
> Winter were lie to me—
> Because I see New Englandly.

It follows from this first assumption, that my ideas will be experienced by each of you from your unique perspective, your history, and

[1] Martha Dickinson and Alfred Leete Hampson, editors. *The Poems of Emily Dickinson.* Boston: Little, Brown, & Co., 1941. p. 307.

your set of beliefs. Fortunately, to some extent our language, our history as educators, our commonality of interests, and those aspects of our culture which we hold in common, should make it possible for you to understand me and for me to shape my ideas so that they will have meaning to you. Yet, it seems clear to me that this expected understanding will be a tenuous connection. We tend to ignore much of the lack of understanding that exists in our daily communication; mutual understanding takes patience, time, and willingness to listen and question.

What does my humanistic/phenomenological perspective mean for thinking about learning and curriculum? I cannot talk about "learning" but rather about "a person learning" and specifically, that person learning in a particular context.

The young child-in-the-world is learning to walk, to speak, to cope; to understand and interpret his/her world. Lois Murphy and her associates have studied this complex developmental process in an intensive longitudinal study of 32 children from infancy to adolescence. In her latest book, *Vulnerability, Coping, and Growth*,[2] she describes this process:

> . . . the child is an active, dynamic creature who quietly or noisily tries to select from the environment what satisfies his individual, vegetative, sensory, motor, cognitive, and social needs. The child tries to protect himself or herself from disintegrative reactions to overwhelming or disturbing stimuli and pressures. These are experienced differentially in line with particular sensitivities, vulnerabilities, and checkerboards of weakness and strength in the child, and the particular supports, compensations, or burdens provided by the family.
> Each child struggles to find solutions and out of these struggles and these solutions develops an implicit or explicit view of life as well as of self.

In the process of this development we cannot say that the child does not have "teachers." Parents, friends, strangers, and environment all provide the opportunities for communication, action, exploration, encounters, the expansion of awareness, and the construction and reconstruction of meaning. Emily Dickinson [3] said:

> Experiment to me
> Is everyone I meet.

Children are also being "conditioned" to some of the values and beliefs that surround them at home. I say "some" for I believe children begin at an early age to select or reject various aspects of their environment; not necessarily self-consciously. We cannot underestimate the

---

[2] Lois B. Murphy and Alice E. Moriarty. *Vulnerability, Coping, and Growth from Infancy to Adolescence.* New Haven: Yale University Press, 1976. p. 13.

[3] Dickinson and Hampson, *op. cit.*, p. 27.

complexity and significance of children's learning before they come to school.

I suppose that the educational rationale for schools (overlooking the babysitting and sorting and labeling functions) is that we do not wish to leave children's learning to chance and varied environments. There are, of course, parallel elements in the in-school and out-of-school environments. Both include, in varying quantities, other children, adults, opportunities to explore and act on the environment, opportunities to communicate, and a variety of obstacles, lacks, and constraints.

An examination of what might differ significantly between these two environments suggests that the *teacher* (a specially-trained adult) and the *prepared* nature of the environment are the two elements of importance that distinguish the in-school setting. These two elements are not the same in all schools but both exist in one form or another.

When we place our children in the school setting and examine what people learning in this context are doing, we find they are doing the same things as in their lives before school, that is, using opportunities for communication, action, exploration, encounters, the expansion of awareness, and the construction and reconstruction of meaning. Children are also being "conditioned" to some of the values and beliefs incorporated in the institution.

If there is a valid argument for the school as a necessary educational institution, its value must be in (a) what is "planned" for the environment and (b) what the teacher does.

Planned schooling environments (and home environments) differ considerably in terms of kinds of buildings, materials, and resources.[4] Generally, I believe that a rich environment (varied and plentiful) is better for learning than is a meager environment. But the *kinds* of materials in the environment are a reflection of the values and expectations of the designers (teacher, principal, central office staff, Board of Education). Whatever designs may be in the minds of the upper ranks, it is the classroom teacher who is the final designer of the environment. The teacher rejects, adapts, adds to, and reinterprets what is available. But more importantly, the teacher is also the guide for what will take place in this environment. He/she controls, to a large extent, what the ground rules will be, what is allowed, and generally, what is legitimate in this environment. This is the central issue: What does my perspective imply about what a teacher and a group of children do? About learning and curriculum?

[4] By schooling environments I do not mean the usual classroom or school. The "classroom" as I wish to define it both moves out of the school and brings the outside world in.

In this context my original assumption about each person's unique perspective can be restated as follows: All teachers (human beings), at any moment in time, perceive children and the responsibility of teaching through their individual network of assumptions and beliefs. Critical assumptions and beliefs of teachers deal with at least the following six considerations: (a) What schools are for. (b) What children are like and how they learn. (c) What is important (values). (d) The meaning of knowledge. (e) The nature of our society and the world. (f) Their (the teachers') understanding of the *role* of the teacher. In each of these six areas I will state some beliefs and assumptions that are part of my perception of the teaching-learning transaction.[5]

1. *What are schools for?* . . . for living, learning, and growing, individually *and* in groups. The quality of life and of human transaction in the school is central. I have tried for some time to describe what I mean by the "quality of life" but I must confess, without much success. I have considered some possible indicators: evidence of aesthetic satisfaction on the part of teacher and students, of involvement, of caring relationships, of sharing and of humor; a variety of activities including inquiry, creative, expressive, and recreational activities; engagement with significant themes in human affairs: brotherhood, peace, poverty, love, self-awareness, freedom. (I reject the idea that schools are merely for the production of "output" faster and more efficiently, particularly the output referred to as the "basic skills" which seems to be the major focus these days.)

2. I believe that *children* (and adults, too) *learn* through involvement in and interaction with their environment: searching, selecting, experimenting, assimilating, and making meaning. (Yet all these action words do not do justice to the remarkable complexity of the learning process. We all have experienced the periods of intense involvement that may alternate with periods of resistance, the shifting rhythms of our activity and focus, and the changing perceptions, attitudes, and desires that are part of the ongoing learning process. One cannot reduce this whole and changing gestalt to a list of actions or a simple definition.)

3. *What is important* to me as a teacher? The primary value I hold is that people are important: I care about their ideas, their feelings, and their needs. I am committed to supporting their growth and well-being. (I must often examine if I merely "think" this value is primary for me,

[5] For some details, see: James B. Macdonald, Bernice Wolfson, and Esther Zaret. *Reschooling Society*. Washington, D.C.: Association for Supervision and Curriculum Development, 1973.

or if I do indeed feel and act on this belief.) A second value I work toward is liberation. I want to enhance awareness of choice and responsibility and to oppose acts that are oppressive. I also value pluralism, desiring to encourage the uniqueness of each human being and oppose efforts to standardize people. I desire to cherish the diversity of human beings and expand my own awareness of the pleasure of this variety. I value participation as an important aspect of learning. Opportunities for decision making and active involvement contribute to the personal significance of the learning experience.

Finally, I value growth and self-realization as important processes I want to support. I must specify the meaning I attach to these words since many different interpretations are available. I do not interpret growth as development, nor as advancement along some linear continuum of skills or grade levels. The process of learning does not, metaphorically speaking, allow us to mount a ladder one equi-distant step after another. Rather, it is a process analogous to the amoeba moving out, surrounding, assimilating, digesting, and then moving out in other directions. I also view growth as expanded awareness, as the elaboration of the phenomenological field or as integration at a higher level of complexity. More concretely, I see it as the increasing realization by the individual of his/her capabilities.

4. My assumptions about *the nature of knowledge* are that all knowledge is uncertain, subject to change, and personally constructed.[6] I believe we have not fully grasped the implications for education of this view of knowledge.

Furthermore we have created problems by first separating thinking and feeling and then trying to find ways to integrate them. It must be evident that we cannot feel without thinking (our awareness or interpretations) nor can we think without feeling (our attitudes, emotions, beliefs, and values). We may *focus* on one or the other aspect of our present, because we have already defined these aspects for ourselves. Perhaps we can some day define a different, more appropriate unit of experience. I think Vigotsky's analogy speaks to this point. In *Thought and Language*,[7] he notes that if our purpose is to find out more about water, studying oxygen and hydrogen separately will not help us understand the properties of water. The appropriate smallest unit would be a molecule of water since it retains all the basic properties of the whole.

[6] See: Michael Polanyi and Harry Prosch. *Meaning*. Chicago: University of Chicago Press, 1975.

[7] L. S. Vigotsky. *Thought and Language*. Cambridge, Massachusetts: The MIT Press, 1962. p. 3.

A number of gestalt theorists and therapists have also touched on this issue.[8]

5. As for *assumptions* and *beliefs* about *the world*, I note that these require constant attention and reexamination. Despite the presence of television, which brings much of the world into our homes in great detail and living color, the complexity, diversity, and constant change in today's world, defy our efforts at awareness. Like Alice in Wonderland, we have to run strenuously just to stay in place.

In order to share, but also to expand my perspective, I need to be open to an awareness of other people's perspectives. There are many opportunities through reading, through contact with other people and other places and, at times through the media, to expand one's awareness of other people's perspectives. A brief list of aspects of our changing world might include: (a) New roles of women and men in our society [9]; (b) Perspectives of oppressed groups here and around the world: blacks, minorities, the poor [10]; (c) The depletion of the world's resources [11]; (d) War and inhumanity today: Northern Ireland, South Africa, South America, U.S. migrant workers, child abuse; and (e) Nuclear danger.

I see what a grim list my awareness provides! But I am also aware of past and present contact with literature, poetry, theatre, and dance in enhancing my own becoming. This past week, in particular, my awareness included the autumnal grace of the Alabama countryside with its striking colors, bright sky, and clear air. As a teacher I wish to provide opportunities for awareness and appreciation, for contact with nature, poetry, and the arts, opportunities for expression through words, movement, and painting.

6. Finally, what is *my understanding of my role as a teacher?* All of my continuing exploration of myself and this world is what I bring to my role as "teacher." From my perspective, teaching involves an enactment of my phenomenological assumptions with my students (and others), and my support of them in their exploration of their assumptions, so that we come to appreciate, understand, and care for each other. (This process is more a direction than a point to achieve.) In this trans-

[8] See, for example: Edward Smith, editor. *The Growing Edge of Gestalt Therapy.* New York: Brunner/Mazel, 1976; and Eugene Gendlin. *Experiencing and the Creation of Meaning.* New York: The Free Press of Glencoe, 1962.

[9] Elizabeth Janeway. *Man's World, Woman's Place.* New York: Dell Publishing Co., 1971; and many other new books.

[10] For example, the works of Robert Coles, Piri Thomas, Maya Angelou, and Angela Davis.

[11] E. F. Schumacher. *Small Is Beautiful.* New York: Harper & Row, 1973.

action, *teacher and students together make the curriculum.* For each it is an individual creative process based on their own perception of the world and their own willingness to risk in reaching out as active learners. It is both their being-in-the-world and their becoming.

No doubt many of you will say that this sounds idealistic but neither real nor practical. There are now some interesting examples of efforts being made in this direction. Some are reported in *The Live Classroom* edited by George Brown.[12]

This set of assumptions, and a holistic approach to being-in-the-world also assumes human intention and an active learner. In this framework, talk of method, technique, and skills is irrelevant. In truth, teacher and students *have* skills, as well as their unique individual perspectives. In the process of their joint curriculum-making and active participation they will *become* more aware and more skilled in some particular context.

As Laura Perls [13] has expressed in *The Growing Edge of Gestalt Therapy:*

A gestalt therapist does not use techniques; he applies *himself in* and *to* a situation with whatever professional skill and life experience he has accumulated and integrated. There are as many styles as there are therapists and clients who discover themselves and each other and together invent their relationship.

I have no doubt this concept also applies to teaching and teaching style. When we try to force teachers into standardized patterns we restrict and ultimately destroy the real life of the teacher as a person in the classroom. Insistence on the use of predesigned systems and curriculum packages, which the teacher is expected to "deliver" to learners, also serves to cut off *live* interactions between teachers and students and is incompatible with the view of persons I have described. And, of course, the use of predetermined behavioral objectives with subsequent measurement of results is equally incompatible with this view and indeed irrelevant to the process of learning as I see it.[14]

What then will occur in schooling environments and how will teachers and students create their curriculum? I see the open classroom approach (an inadequate label) with its opportunity for active choice and

---

[12] George I. Brown, editor. *The Live Classroom.* New York: The Viking Press, 1975.

[13] Laura Perls. "Comments on New Directions." In: Edward Smith, editor, *op. cit.,* p. 223.

[14] See: James Macdonald and Bernice J. Wolfson. "A Case Against Behavioral Objectives." *Elementary School Journal* 71: 119-28; December 1970.

responsibility as the appropriate environment for pursuing this joint activity. Persons in such an environment will focus on their being-in-the-world and, in sharing their perspectives, will contribute to the awareness and "becoming" of others, opening new possibilities, new goals, and new involvements.

I am acutely aware of how general and abstract this sounds, so I will try to offer a few specific illustrations.

1. An eight-year-old boy has informed the group that his family has found a new apartment and that he will be leaving soon. Feelings and questions related to this event emerge: He is unhappy to leave his friends. Some of his classmates are unhappy to see him go. Can they visit him? Will he come back? What is his new neighborhood like? How is it different from this one? Why do people move? What does it cost to move? Do you know any people there? What is your new school like?

The choice to pursue any of the above questions is a possibility to be explored and reflected upon.

2. The opportunity to choose to engage in various types of creative expression would always be present. Such activity would be approved, supported, and shared as desired.

3. The larger world of parents, other adults, the community, would be utilized to expand the possibility of exploration, encounter, reflection, and awareness.

Indeed, learning processes do go on in any kind of in-school or out-of-school setting. It is the communicated beliefs and attitudes of the teacher (or other adults) that confirm or disconfirm the being of the child.

I would like to share an artist's description of her own exploration and construction of meaning. It is the most perceptive account I have found. Agnes DeMille [15] in one of her autobiographical books, *And Promenade Home,* said:

But we may be grateful that very seldom are circumstances propitious and that the work fights through hard and slow. The moment one knows how, one begins to die a little. Living is a form of not being sure, of not knowing what next or how. And the artist before all others never entirely knows. He guesses. And he may be wrong. But then how does one know whom to befriend or, for that matter, to marry? One can't go through life on hands and knees. One leaps in the dark. For this reason creative technique reduces itself basically to a recognition and befriending of one's self. "Who am I?" the artist asks, and he devotes his entire career to answering.

[15] Agnes DeMille. *And Promenade Home.* Boston: Little, Brown & Co., 1958. pp. 190-91. Reprinted by permission of Harold Ober Associates Incorporated. Copyright © 1956, 1957, 1958 by Agnes DeMille.

There is one clue: what moves him is his. What amuses or frightens or pleases him becomes by virtue of his emotional participation a part of his personality and history; conversely what neither moves nor involves him, what brings him no joy, can be reckoned as spurious. An artist begins to go wrong exactly at the point where he begins to pretend. But it is difficult sometimes to accept the truth. He has to learn who he in fact is, not who he would like to be, nor even who it would be expedient or profitable to be.

In my view the teacher and the artist, and indeed all students, are engaged in the same search and it is the teacher's role to encourage students to join in creating the curriculum to enhance their being-in-the-world and to facilitate their becoming (learning). It is a lively and lifelong vocation.

Part V

Sociopolitical Analysis and Curriculum Theory

Dwayne Huebner attempts to find a basis for applying the work of Karl Marx to human development. He analyzes and compares the work of Piaget in child development to that of Marx in economic theory and finds that both ground their work in human activity. In attempting to sketch out the boundaries of what he refers to as genetic Marxism, Huebner argues that we do not need more studies. What we need, he suggests, is "consciousness of our own complicity in the forces of domination, and a critical methodology which will inform and be informed by our practice as educators."

Michael W. Apple and Nancy King set out to develop a conceptual scheme that will allow them to examine what is taught in schools and why some social meanings are used as a basis for organizing school life while others are excluded. They reject Silberman's thesis that schools are the way they are because of mindlessness. Apple and King describe what is commonly labeled the hidden curriculum as the mechanism by which schools reproduce the cultural assumptions and class relationships of capitalist America.

10. Toward a Political Economy of Curriculum and Human Development

Dwayne Huebner

The writings of Marx and his followers have too infrequently informed the concerns of the curriculum person and those in related educational fields. The social-political reasons for this under-utilization are obvious, inasmuch as the class analysis of the 30's and of this recent critical period were often interpreted as being subversive of U.S. political and economic institutions. However, the philosophical-historical reasons are less obvious, and worthy of significant scholarship, for the historical, dialectical, and material content of his writings describe phenomena which can be interpreted as educational. This paper is intended as a pointer to some of the issues and possibilities which might be considered if a curriculum person were to engage in the critical interpretation of the writings of Marx and his followers. I claim no special competency for this task except interest and a home base in this presumed field of curriculum.

The historical task is a major one if we are to understand why the writings of Marx have been ignored by educators of the United States, except those brave few, some of whom have suffered the consequences. I presume that the reason, in part, revolves around two major figures at the turn of the century, plus or minus twenty years or so—Harris and Dewey. The Hegelianism of Harris had no small impact upon the character of schooling in the United States. Cremin[1] credits Harris with

[1] Lawrence Cremin. "Curriculum Making in the United States." *Teachers College Record* 64: 196-200; January 1971.

establishing the basic paradigm of the curriculum field which prevails today with minor themes and variations. Perhaps even more important is his impact on the organization of the schools and his concern for textbooks as the center of the curriculum, rather than the teacher as the center. Although one American Hegelian, August Willich,[2] was a colleague of Marx and Engels, the Fuerbachian and Marxian critique and surpassing of Hegel did not make much of an impact on the other American Hegelians. Crucial in this historical picture is Dewey's encounter with Hegel by way of G. S. Morris at Johns Hopkins[3] and his turn to pragmatism. I am unfamiliar with whether Dewey's pragmatism is in part founded by a critical reaction to Marx. However, it is fascinating that both Dewey and Marx cut a philosophical eyetooth or two on Hegel. For reasons perhaps best explained by Novak,[4] Dewey's particular pragmatic surpassing of Hegel dominated educational thought to the exclusion of other post-Hegelian philosophies. It seems that the 60 years before the publication of Bobbitt's *Curriculum*[5] might be as important for understanding our intellectual ground as the 60 years following it.

There have been those students of education who have utilized Marx's ideas of *Das Kapital* to analyze the place of schooling in our economic and political structure. In the 1920's and 30's Langford[6] and Slesinger[7] stand out, and in this critical period the works of Mann[8] and Bowles and Gintis[9] are notable. The analysis has been at the macro level. Concepts of class, labor, alienation, commodity, capital accumulation, and imperialism have been used to describe how schools and other structures of education reproduce the labor force and class distinctions within the capitalistic economy and the political and social institutions which accompany it. These macro analyses have called our attention to the controlling functions inherent in institutionalized educational structures, and point out the masking function of much past and present cur-

[2] William H. Goetzman, editor. *The American Hegelians*. New York: Alfred A. Knopf, 1973.

[3] *Ibid.*

[4] George Novak. *Pragmatism Versus Marxism: An Appraisal of John Dewey's Philosophy*. New York: Pathfinder Press, 1975.

[5] Franklin Bobbitt. *The Curriculum*. Boston: Houghton Mifflin Company, 1918.

[6] Howard Langford. *Education and Social Conflict*. New York: Macmillan, 1935.

[7] Zalmen Slesinger. *Education and the Class Struggle*. New York: Couici-Friedo, 1937.

[8] John S. Mann. "Influences of Marxism on Curriculum Theory." Paper presented to Professors of Curriculum, New Orleans, April 1976.

[9] Samuel Bowles and Herbert Gintis. *Schooling in Capitalist America*. New York: Basic Books, 1975.

ricular language which proclaims the school's presumed role in "self-realization" and a more perfect "democratic" society.

With few exceptions in this country, the writings of Marx have not been used to explore the micro aspects of education—the interpersonal or intersubjective—the biography of the individual within specific social locations. One of the reasons for this is given by Joel Kovel,[10] who writes of the dialectical relationship between Freud and Marx. He suggests that Marx, to accomplish his great achievement, necessarily had to be concerned with only those aspects of human life that could be objectified and hence become a commodity. In effect, Marx had to bracket the subjective in order to explain the objective. Kovel suggests that Freud had to bracket the objective in order to deal with the subjective—the interpersonal and fantasy. Because Marx did not attend to the interpersonal and the subjective, the application of his ideas to the evolving biography of the individual within the prevailing objective structures is difficult, although some neo-Marxists have made the effort.[11] Reich [12] has described the dialectical relation between the economic-political structure and the sexual life of individuals. Horkheimer,[13] in his work on the family, has illustrated how the family mediates between the economic structures and the life of the child. He shows how the relations of production carry into the home, thus producing the individual who fits into the capitalistic structures. Today, I suppose that it would be equally easy to show how the commodity structure and consumerism work their way into the home, not only via the activity of the parents, but by the mass medium of TV, the commodity which carries the image of all other commodities into the bedroom or kitchen. These mediating structures of home and media are surely important vehicles for describing how the forces and relations of production and the market impinge upon the child.

The historical dialectical method of Marx, developed in the mid-19th century, must be interpreted·historically and dialectically. The genetic epistemology of Piaget,[14] no matter how flawed or partial, is part of the totality to be considered as the methods and rhetoric of Marx are reinter-

[10] Joel Kovel. "The Marxist View of Man and Psychoanalysis." *Social Research* 45:220-45; Summer 1976.

[11] Richard Lichtman. "Marx and Freud." *Socialist Revolution* 30: 3-56; October-December 1976.

[12] Wilhelm Reich. *The Invasion of Compulsory Sex-Morality.* New York: Farrar, Straus and Giroux, 1971.

[13] Max Horkheimer. "Authority and the Family." *Critical Essays.* Matthew O'Connor, translator. New York: Herder & Herder, 1972.

[14] Jean Piaget. *Biology and Knowledge.* Chicago: University of Chicago Press, 1971.

preted in the situation of today. The significance which most educators attach to the work of Piaget, namely that he describes the cognitive functioning of the individual during different stages of growth, is, for my purposes, a masking of Piaget's more important contribution. Piaget has described the evolution, in the epistemic subject, of logico-mathematical structures. Piaget's work suggests that the adult decenter. Mathematics is not only what the adult does when computing and operating in science laboratories or in industry. Mathematics is also what the child does when he/she groups objects, orders objects according to various attributes, and engages in a host of other transforming activities in the world. Piaget calls our attention to a different definition of knowledge structures. No longer can we see knowledge as finished form built into the behavior of adults and their tools which must then be "taught" to the child. Piaget has asked us to see knowledge structures as evolving—if you wish, as biographical or historical and as dialectical. Whereas Marx has forced us to see ideologies and social, economic, and political structures within an historical and dialectical focus, Piaget has accomplished the same thing from the perspective of the history of involvement of the individual. Whereas Piaget has attended primarily to the logico-mathematical, and indeed has clearly bracketed out of his consideration metaphysical and ideological knowledge, he makes possible a genetic culture. He brings into our awareness the possibility that all adult forms of knowing and action can be, should be, seen in the perspective of their genesis in the person. No longer should we adults be permitted to see adult forms of knowledge or action as *the* way to interpret knowledge or action. Just as Marx required that we see them as social phenomena, and interpret them historically and dialectically, so Piaget asks that we now see them genetically (or historically) and dialectically in the individual person.

The Piagetian task confronting Marxism is to identify and describe the forms or structures of a "genetic" Marxism. How does Marxism, as a structure of social action and thought, evolve and become distorted in an individual? It is normally assumed that Marxism is an adult framework for viewing and acting in adult social life, and that the tasks of the Marxist are to develop the class consciousness and political organization of the proletariat to fulfill its historic mission. Given this charge, the Marxist educator must disseminate the political-economic tools for analysis and reconstruction of social life. The use of Marxian tools demystifies the forces of domination, builds political leadership, and develops the class consciousness necessary to mobilize political action of large segments of the people. This is the tack of Bowles and Gintis [15] in

---

[15] Bowles and Gintis, *op. cit.*

education; and indeed it is an important one, whether one shares their political commitments or not.

But if we had a genetic Marxism, the questions of the educator would be different. Assume that Marxian "revolutionary practice" has as its origins biological and social givens and activities of the infant. If the continuities and the discontinuities of this evolving operational structure can be identified, then perhaps we can see how the social and material environment intrudes upon or facilitates the development of so-called mature Marxian thought and action.[16]

This is what I wish to point to in this paper. I do not hope to accomplish the task in the paper, but merely to point to needed and possible intellectual work. If we can move toward this goal of a "genetic" Marxism, then I think that we can also move toward a political economy of the curriculum and of human development itself. We should then depict more precisely the various mediations between the neophyte and the adult world, not with the intent of improving our educational control over the child, but with the possibility of pointing out the educational significance of the child for the adult, and the need to construct more effective means for producing appropriate qualities of life for young and old.

The first task, then, is to map the intellectual tools of Marxism. The function of mapping these tools, these intellectual operations, is to provide a point of origin for genetic analysis. My operation is indeed abstract and conceptual, with the full recognition that the only appropriate method is finally phenomenological and dialectical, which entails bringing to consciousness the child-adult relationship over time—an autobiography of social relations.

The extensiveness, complexity, and detail of Marx's writings make the mapping task almost foolhardy. One is tempted to use already existing maps, such as Ollman's fine work on *Alienation*.[17] But a map is a tool, an instrument of production. Even an intellectual tool or means of production one must own, in order that the production has use value for the person. Thus, in my beginning appropriation of Marx's language tools personal choices are made, with the full recognition that if my production is to have social use value it must become part of the social dialectic, and hence critiqued and negated or surpassed by others.

As a point of origin for this particular activity I would identify the following as significant markers: activity, work, labor, labor power;

[16] Karl Marx. "Theses on Feuerbach." *The German Ideology*. New York: International Publishers, 1947. pp. 195-99.

[17] Bertell Ollman. *Alienation*. Cambridge: Cambridge University Press, 1971.

means of production, property; use-value, exchange-value, commodity; relations of production; alienation, class and class consciousness; surplus value and capital. However, here I shall be concerned only with activity, work, labor, labor power; means of production; and relations of production. My tactic will be to point in the direction that I think a genetic Marxism might take, and to suggest the direction of possible implications for curriculum and the way that we adults might talk about child-adult relations over time.

Marx begins his analysis of Capitalism in Volume I of *Das Kapital* [18] with the commodity and commodity exchange, but central to his analysis is the labor process. Labor is the process by which nature is appropriated for individual and social use and by means of which use-value is produced. The productive process, which is at the same time a process of consumption, requires means of production—the instruments of production and the subject of production: property. Specialization of labor leads gradually to a separation of the laboring process from the ownership of the means of production, hence the selling of one's labor power and the alienation of one's own being from one's labor and the products of this labor. Capital as surplus labor results, and hence the class distinctions between those who own property and have capital and those who have only their labor power as a commodity to exchange for other commodities. Labor, then, is central to any understanding of Marx's writing, and is a key language tool for his economic and political analysis. What are the origins of labor in the person? Or to use Piagetian language, how can genesis of labor be described in the biography of the person and how can its origins be detected in the activity of the young child? Under what circumstances in one's life history does the alienation of labor occur, and when does the person begin to see his/her labor as labor for someone else, as something to be exchanged? Who owns the means of production in the life of the child? How does that ownership contribute to alienation and the loss or increase of power to produce one's own quality of life and to participate willingly in the social production of life? [19]

Marx states that "Labour is, in the first place, a process in which both man and Nature participate, and in which man of his own accord starts, regulates, and controls the material reactions between himself and Nature." [20] In *A Contribution to a Critique of Political Economy* he states that "In the process of production, members of society appropriate

[18] Karl Marx. *Capital: A Critique of Political Economy. Volume I: The Process: Capitalist Production.* Frederick Engels, editor. New York: International, 1967.

[19] Cf. Lichtman on this point.

[20] Marx, *Capital*, p. 177.

(produce, fashion) natural products in accordance with human requirements" [21] and "Production is always appropriation of nature by an individual within and with the help of a definite social organization." [22] For Marx, "The elementary factors of the labor process are (a) the personal activity of man, i.e., work itself; (b) the subject of that work; and (c) its instruments." [23] Within the many writings of Marx, Ollman indicates how Marx gradually shifts from the term "activity" to the term "work." Productive activity is work. Ollman claims that "For Marx, labor is always alienated productive activity." [24]

It is at this point that the specific content of Piaget's writing becomes helpful, not simply his methodology and general commitment to genetic epistemology. There seems to be a striking similarity between Marx and Piaget with respect to significance of activity and the appropriation of nature. You will recall that Piaget grounds logical-mathematical knowledge in the schemata of action.[25] He claims that knowledge and intelligence are transformations of the world, dependent upon the schemata of assimilation and accommodation. For Piaget, as for Marx, the significant aspect of human life is active interchange with the environment from which Piaget draws his genetic conceptions of knowledge and Marx his historical conceptions of labor, alienation, and capital. The foundation of knowledge for Piaget is the body and the biological determinants of the schemata of assimilation and accommodation. The foundation of the social-economic-political structure for Marx is also the material structure of the body in the world (in fact Marx refers to Nature as "man's inorganic body" [26]) from which develops, historically, our ideologies, knowledge structures, and social relations. The basic "instruments" of activity for Piaget are the schemata which are founded in the biological structures. The instruments of activity for Marx are the means of production, property. Thus, indicating the basic material base upon which they both ground their work.

The obvious hunch at this stage of the interpretation is that Piaget's schemata of action are the subjective correlates of Marx's objective means of production. In fact, Marx, referring to "the factors of the labor process," calls attention to "its objective factors, the means of produc-

[21] Karl Marx. *A Contribution to the Critique of Political Economy.* Maurice Dobb, editor. New York: International Publishers, 1970. p. 193.

[22] *Ibid.*, p. 192.

[23] Marx, *Capital*, p. 178.

[24] Ollman, *Alienation*, p. 171.

[25] Piaget, *Biology and Knowledge.*

[26] Karl Marx. *The Economic and Philosophic Manuscripts of 1844.* Dirk Struik, editor. New York: International Publishers, 1964. p. 110.

tion, as well as its subjective factors, labor power." [27] The schemata and means of production are not only instruments, but become or are vehicles which support activity, give it direction or intentionality, and increase its power. The use of the word "power" is significant, for Marx refers to "labor-power" as the commodity that the laborer exchanges for wages. Surplus labor-power, the labor-power beyond that needed for the maintenance and reproduction of the laborer himself/herself, is the source of surplus value, the source of capital. Surplus labor power, rather than being consumed for social production or for production of the laborer— going beyond his/her own reproduction to produce new personal qualities of life and activity—is used to produce wealth for someone else.

Marx and Piaget both recognize that activity itself produces the person as well as transforms the world or produces use-value in the social world. Whereas this is readily seen in the works of Piaget, it stands forth less clearly in the more common interpretations of Marx. Marx states quite specifically that the person "opposes himself to Nature as one of her own forces, setting in motion arms and legs, head and hands, the natural forces of his body, in order to appropriate Nature's productions in a form adapted to his own wants. By this acting on the external world and changing it, he at the same time changes his own nature. He develops his slumbering powers and compels them to act in obedience to his sway." [28]

Thus, both Marx and Piaget ground their work in human activity, which is exhibited at birth. Activity is the manifestation of human life and the starting point of our concern. In *The Economic and Philosophic Manuscripts of 1844*, Marx asked "what is life but activity?" [29] We need not dig beneath the surface to infer motive or biological explanations of activity for purposes of understanding education, although clearly such digging is interesting and valuable. The infant exhibits undifferentiated activity. How is that activity gradually differentiated and focused? How does the stuff of the social-material world shape activity and give it power and direction? Under what circumstances does activity cease being activity for one's self and become activity for another, that is, when does it become alienated labor? In thinking through answers to these questions, both Piaget and Marx are helpful; for Piaget attends to the body, specifically to the cognitive, dimensions of some of the answers, whereas Marx attends to the social and property dimensions of some of the answers. Thus we have pointed, so far, to the genetic origins of labor

[27] Marx, *Capital*, p. 184.
[28] *Ibid.*, p. 177.
[29] Marx, *Economic and Philosophic Manuscripts*, p. 111.

and to the possible significance of the means of production in this genetic labor.

We have also called attention, although much too briefly, to the notion of labor power and the significance of power in human life. As educators, we have been more inclined to talk of the person in terms of needs rather than powers, and we have been inclined to speak of needs assessments or deficiencies rather than how a person uses his/her power. But the focus of labor power suggests that we begin to ask how children use their surplus energy, beyond that needed for self-maintenance. To what extent do they recognize the power to construct, to produce new qualities of life for themselves, and to produce new qualities of life, new environments for others? To what extent is that surplus energy seen as something negative, to be feared, repressed, or sublimated, or used by others; as a source of guilt because it comes up against, and perhaps brings judgments against, the already established which others seek to maintain? In the course of a person's life, when is surplus energy seen as "labor power," a commodity to be exchanged for other commodities? But before these points can be elaborated, we must attend to the social dimension and to the genesis of the relations of production.

Again, Marx is quite clear as to the social dimension in his writings. The significance of social class and class consciousness is the obvious indicator of this social dimension. In the *Grundrisse* he states that: "Each individual's production is dependent on the production of others" and that "private interest is already a socially determined interest." [30] In a sense, then, activity for Marx is always social activity, although the social dimension is often hidden by the alienation of labor and commodities. For Piaget, the social dimension is more opaque. In spite of defining cognition as founded on operations which connect the agent and the environment, he fails to ground his cognition of the child in the operations which exist between himself, the experimenter, and the child. It is interesting that as Piaget speaks of the physicist and physics, he states that "the physicist constantly acts, and the first thing he does is to transform objects and phenomena in order to get at the laws validating these transformations." [31] Yet he appears not to acknowledge his own acts. His very knowledge about cognitive development in the young is a consequence of his action; he has transformed the relationships between the child and his environment by manipulating objects, asking questions, or placing puzzles or tasks before the child. His stages of cognitive devel-

[30] Karl Marx. *Grundrisse.* David McLellan, editor and translator. New York: Harper & Row, 1971.

[31] Piaget, *Biology and Knowledge*, p. 338.

opment are social, a consequence of his very intervention into the life of the child, and participation in the activity of the child. Piaget's conceptions of the intellectual development of the child are not only conceptions of the intellectual development of the child, but also of the development of the social relationship between the child and the experimenter, in which the social activity of the adult is masked or taken for granted. The correctives against forgetting or masking the activity of the adult are two. First, a phenomenological methodology would help, in which the investigator brackets out his/her own taken-for-granted realities and indeed turns to consciousness of the "thing itself." The thing itself in the Piagetian experiment is not the child and his/her environment, but the child, the material environment, and the social environment consisting of the child and the experimenter, which necessarily includes the language activity between them. The other corrective is the empirical literature which seeks to describe the genesis of the social relationship between the neonate and the caregiver. The role or activity of the experimenter must also be reflected upon in this empirical work.

A speculative overview of the problem is found in Macmurray's *Persons in Relations*,[32] wherein the infant is described as a rational person at birth. A person is not an isolated individual, but can exist only in relation with others. For Macmurray, the child supplies the motives, the caregiver supplies the intentions; the combination of intention and motive means rationality. The infant can live only through or by means of communication; communication does not develop through life with another. Language, then, is a consequence of communication, not vice versa. Social relations are foundational for the continuation of individual life.

An empirical approach to the problem is found in *The Effect of the Infant on Its Caregiver*,[33] edited by Lewis and Rosenblum. The studies which they brought together were intended to support the thesis of the editors that: "Not only is the infant or child influenced by its social, political, economic, and biological world, but in fact the child itself influences its world in turn." [34] The editors demonstrate with empirical findings that which Marx has demonstrated by way of his dialectical materialism and Piaget by his genetic epistemology—that the activity

[32] John Macmurray. *Persons in Relations*. New York: Harper & Bros., 1961. Chapter II.

[33] Michael Lewis and Leonard Rosenblum. *The Effect of the Infant on Its Caregiver*. New York: John Wiley & Sons, 1974.

[34] *Ibid.*, "Introduction," p. xv.

between the person and the world, even the social world, produces the person and transforms the world. In the volume Bell refers to the fact "that both parent and offspring behave so as to produce or maintain the behavior of the other." [35] The various studies point to the mutual significance of facial, vocal, and gaze behaviors in which the infant is often the instigator and terminator of a series of interactions. In a report on the relationship between blind infants and their mothers, Fraiberg describes how the absence of the infant's gaze changes typical mothering reactions, and alters vocalization patterns of mother and infant. Compensation for this lack of visual contact is possible if the mother is helped to respond vocally to the movement cues of the infant, and if tactile replaces visual communication and eye play.[36]

Additional information is provided in *Temperament and Behavior Disorders* by Thomas and others, in which the authors identify temperament as a crucial factor in the development of behavior disorders. They hypothesize that the "behavioral style of the individual child . . . the characteristic tempo, rhythmicity, adaptability, energy expenditure, mood, and focus of attention" [37] of a child is a key factor in understanding the social interactions of the child. I interpret this to mean that the physiological characteristics of the individual organism impact on the evolving social relations between the child and his/her caregivers. It seems reasonable to generalize beyond Piaget here. Piaget claims that the logico-mathematical schemata which serve as "specialized organs of regulation in the control of exchanges with the environment" [38] are founded on the biological structures of the child. It would be reasonable to hypothesize that schemata also evolve which serve as organs of regulation in the control of exchanges with other persons, and that these are grounded in biological structures of the infant, hence the significance of temperament in social relationships and their distortions. However, it does not seem reasonable to use the expression assimilation and accommodation with respect to these presumed schemata of regulation in the exchange with others, unless we add the qualifier "negotiated" assimilation and "negotiated" accommodation, for the mutuality of impact and the mutuality of self-production must be acknowledged.

[35] Richard Bell. "Contributions of Human Infants to Caregiving and Social Interaction," Lewis and Rosenblum, pp. 1-30.

[36] Selma Fraiburg. "Blind Infants and Their Mothers: An Examination of the Sign System," Lewis and Rosenblum, pp. 215-32.

[37] Alexander Thomas *et al. Temperament and Behavior Disorder in Children.* New York: New York University Press, 1968.

[38] Piaget, *Biology and Knowledge*, p. 354.

I have suggested a parallel between environmental interactions and social interactions, using Piaget formulations of the logico-mathematical as the metaphor. I wish to carry this parallel one step further, in order to get to a potentially more useful handle on the problem of social relations, the relation of production, and the phenomena of consciousness. Piaget states that "to attribute logic and mathematics to the general coordinates of the subject's action . . . is a recognition of the fact that while the fecundity of the subject's thought process depends on the internal resources of the organism, the efficacy of those processes depends on the fact that the organism is not independent of the environment but can only live, act, or think in interaction with it." [39] Piaget's overall strategy was to begin with the givenness of mathematics and scientific knowledge and to search for their origins in the child. In so doing he has also, of course, reconstructed our knowledge of these disciplines. But he did not start with general notions of schemata of assimilation and accommodation and then find that they led to logico-mathematical formal structures.

The parallel I would suggest is that the forms of language usage are the coordinates of social relations, and that the clues to the possible schemata of these social relations are to be found in the functions of speech between and among persons in their many relations. The work of Merleau-Ponty, a phenomenologist, supports this parallel. He describes speech as an extension of the body, in a sense affirming that both logico-mathematical operations and speech are founded in biological givens. He states that "language is a manifestation, a revelation of intimate being and of the psychic link which unites us to the world and to our fellow man." [40] Later he claims that,

There is one particular culture object which is destined to play a crucial role in the perception of other people: language. In dialogue there is constituted between the other person and myself a common ground: my thought and his are woven into a single fabric, my words and those of my interlocutor are called forth by the state of the discussion, and they are inserted into a shared operation of which neither of us is the creator. We have here a dual being, where the other is for me no longer a mere bit of behavior in my transcendental field, nor I in his; we are collaborators for each other in consummate reciprocity. [41]

Paralleling Piaget's reflective abstraction whereby the logico-mathematical structures are constructed, Merleau-Ponty writes that, "It is only

[39] *Ibid.*, p. 345.

[40] Maurice Merleau-Ponty. *The Phenomenology of Perception.* Colin Smith, translator. London: Routledge & Kegan Paul, 1962.

[41] *Ibid.*, p. 354.

retrospectively, when I have withdrawn from the dialogue and am recall-ing it that I am able to integrate it into my life and make it an episode in my private history." [42]

The work of Kohlberg fails to be informed by the methods of phenomenology and the work of Merleau-Ponty. In fact, he misses the fundamental contribution of Piaget in this respect—that knowledge and formal operations are grounded in action. Kohlberg has merely estab-lished stages of potential inauthentic or alienated discourse about moral activity. His failure to ground the evolution of moral discourse in the evolving social relations of individuals, in their coordinates of social action, is a major fault of his work.

The studies of the interaction between infant and caregiver indicate that the infant is born into a social relationship, and indeed partakes in the structuring of the interactive patterns which make up that social relation. Some of the early studies of language development point to the fact that the communicative relationship between caregivers and infant is foundational for the establishment of dialogue and language. We have inferred from this that the functions of speech in dialogue, the forms that language takes between and among individuals, are reflective of the schemata of social relations. Stated from the other side, social relations are constitutive of language functions. That which needs to be traced empirically and phenomenologically is the gradual transition from these social relations of care and communication to the relations of production. Furthermore, if the above hunches are correct it should also be possible to detect the shifts in the language exchanges as these gradually express the language of production. Much of the empirical work probably exists. It is obvious, and indeed the work of Horkheimer [43] and Schneider [44] suggests, that the dynamics of family life begin to assume the shape of the relations of production. Horkheimer has shown how the hierarchy of authority in work-places carries over to the authority structures in family, and hence reproduces in children attitudes and behavior which are required for the work force. The sexual liberation movements of today have also called attention to the penetration of family dynamics by the hierarchical and stereotypical structures in business, industry, and other places of adult occupation. Likewise, it seems rather common knowledge among teachers that the language of the classroom readily and quickly assumes the form of the language of production, with em-

[42] Ibid.

[43] Horkheimer, "Authority and the Family."

[44] Michael Schneider. Neurosis and Civilization, A Marxist/Freudian Synthesis. Michael Roloff, translator. New York: Seabury Press, 1975.

phasis on production (what one has learned) and external authority. The recent work on communication competence and distorted communication is a possible source of further data and methodologies for exploring the relationships among language functions, social relations, and the relations of production.[45]

The centrality of language in a genetic Marxism is also indicated by the significance of language for consciousness. In *The German Ideology* Marx states that "Language is as old as consciousness, language is practical consciousness. . . . Consciousness is therefore from the very beginning a social product." [46] Later he claims "that the real intellectual wealth of the individual depends entirely on the wealth of his real connections." [47] I am not certain what he intends by the words "intellectual wealth," but for me it entails consciousness. Again, in education we have been so conditioned to think of the individual and his/her consciousness, his/her language, that we fail to recognize the social and relational aspect of that consciousness and that language. Thus, it is less a matter of changing one's language patterns, of changing his/her consciousness of who he/she is, than of changing his/her relations with others, and broadening this range of relationships. It seems to me that psychotherapy illustrates this, for by working through a significant relationship with the therapist, the client speaks differently about him/herself and others, and has a changed consciousness about him/herself in the world. Hence class consciousness is necessarily a creation of dialectical thinking and awareness. Class consciousness exists when one recognizes those with whom he/she is in relation and those with whom he/she has few or distorted relations, perhaps indeed only relations of production, consumption, or exchange.

Some of the implications of this analysis for curriculum and our "understanding" of human development are easy to generate. If we take seriously the possibility of a genetic Marxism, then further inquiry might produce more useful knowledge about the dialectical relationship between adults, the structures of the adult world, and the child. Central to such inquiry would not be cognition or affect, but the shape of human activity throughout the lifetime of the person, the developing power of the person for self and social production, the evolving social relations of the person, the relationship of self activity to social activity, the evolving

---

[45] Jurgen Habermas. "Toward a Theory of Communicative Competence." *Recent Sociology.* Volume 2. Hans Peter Dreitzel, editor. New York: Macmillan, 1970. pp. 114-49.

[46] Marx, *German Ideology*, p. 19.

[47] *Ibid.*, p. 27.

functions of language as manifestations of social relations and consciousness, including class consciousness, the functions of production and ownership, and use-value of the materials of production for children, the relationships of these materials to the schemata of assimilation and accommodation of the child, and the relationship of these materials to the productive forces within the society.

Inquiry into such phenomena is part of our problem, for it is a division of labor which produces elites and develops not consciousness, but knowledge, which becomes a commodity to be exchanged for degrees, salary increments, tenure, promotion, royalties, and privilege. As Marx said in his last thesis on Feuerbach: "The philosophers have only *interpreted* the world; the point is, to *change* it." [48]

We really do not need more studies; we need consciousness of our own complicity in the forces of domination, and a critical methodology which will inform and be informed by our practice as educators. That critical methodology and practice is social, dialectical, and materialistic. By social I mean only that individuality is only possible because we are, have been, and will be in relation with others; and that our fundamental concern is and must be the quality of that social life. Infants and young children partake of our social being. The unfortunate question as to how they become socialized hides that fact. Only our naive and extreme individualism lets us speak of earning a living so we can raise children, rather than producing a life for ourselves and others. Our activity and that of the young is part of the continuing transformation of energy and material for the sake of our collective life. To have that activity turned into alienated activity, for someone else rather than for the person and the collective which he/she chooses, is the beginning of distortion of the social relations, of domination, and of language which no longer expresses truth and possibility.

By "dialectical" I mean seeing the part in terms of the totality, the present in terms of the past and the future, and recognizing that contradictions are also a mode of relationship which offer as much understanding of the present moment as cause and effect relationships. The child is a part of our whole, a significant part of our past, present, and future, and a source of some of our major contradictions. To speak of adult life without the presence of children is an absurdity; and that absurdity is demonstrated by our efforts to wall them off from our everydayness as adults in schools—public school, preschool, church school, and what have you. Walling them off means that we never have to ask what they mean for us and how much of our productive power

[48] Marx, "Theses on Feuerbach," p. 199.

should be used for their life. We only need ask what we mean for them, and what they must learn, how they must be socialized, how they will inherit our wealth. Dialectical method and practice require that we see the life of the child against the lives of the adults, the activity of children in classrooms against the activities of adults in automobile production plants, banana plantations, cocktail lounges at the top of the World Trade Center, the pushers in Harlem, the prisoners and guards in Attica, and in faculty meetings. The contradictions seen and felt will never be reduced by a curriculum, but are the source of consciousness, of class consciousness.

By "materialistic" I intend a concern for the body—the body of the person and the body of the world, and the respect that is due both. Productive interchange between the two is necessary for life. The instruments that have been fashioned to direct this interchange, and to increase life's power, can be respectful or disrespectful of the body of the person and the body of the world, for the instruments that have been fashioned can indeed alienate individuals, increase collective power, or rape the body of the world. The instruments which have become tools of education are often disrespectful of both, used for profit-making, for developing impotence and social weakness, or for producing laborers to do the work of and for others. The schemata of assimilation and accommodation are often for the appropriation of the body of the world for the few; even the public materials for education are often designed for only private gain.

If there is indeed a political economy of the curriculum and of child development, it will not tell us how to educate young people but how the young and the old can live together for mutual benefit and how the current structures of production and consumption intrude upon the social relations among people, young and old, near and far, rich and poor, black and white.

11. What Do Schools Teach?*

Michael W. Apple and Nancy R. King

Schooling and Cultural Capital

One of the least attractive arguments in recent years has been that schools are relatively unexciting, boring, or what have you, because of mindlessness.[1] The argument has it that schools covertly teach all those things that humanistic critics of schools so like to write and talk about—behavioral consensus, institutional rather than personal goals and norms, alienation from one's products—because teachers, administrators, and other educators do not really know what they are doing. However, such a perspective is misleading at best. In the first place, it is thoroughly ahistorical. It ignores the fact that schools were in part designed to teach exactly these things. The hidden curriculum, the tacit teaching of social and economic norms and expectations to students in schools, was not as hidden or "mindless" as many educators believe. Second, it ignores the critical task schools perform as the fundamental set of institutions in advanced industrial societies that certifies adult competence. It pulls schools out of their setting within a larger and much more powerful nexus of economic and political institutions that give schools their meaning. That is, schools seem to do what they are in fact supposed to do,

---

* Expanded versions of this paper appear in: Richard Weller, editor. *Humanistic Education.* Berkeley, California: McCutchan Publishing Corp., 1977; and in: *Curriculum Inquiry* 6(4):341-68; 1977.

[1] Charles Silberman. *Crisis in the Classroom.* New York: Random House, 1970.

at least in terms of roughly providing dispositions and propensities that are quite functional to one's later life in a complex and stratified social and economic order.

While there is no doubt that mindlessness does exist besides in Charles Silberman's mind, it is not an adequate descriptive device—nor is venality or indifference—in explaining why schools are so resistant to change or why schools teach what they do.[2] Nor is it an appropriate conceptual tool to ferret out what exact kinds of things are taught in schools or why certain social meanings and not others are used to organize school life. Yet it is not just the school critics who are a bit too simple in their analysis of the social and economic meaning of schools.

All too often the social meaning of school experience has been accepted as unproblematic by sociologists of education or as merely engineering problems by curriculum specialists and other programmatically inclined educators. The curriculum field especially, among other educational areas, has been dominated by a perspective that might best be called "technological" in that the major interest guiding its work has involved finding the one best set of means to reach pre-chosen educational ends.[3] Against this relatively ameliorative and uncritical background, a number of sociologists and curriculum scholars, influenced strongly by the sociology of knowledge in both its Marxist or "Neo-Marxist" and phenomenological variants, have begun to raise serious questions about this lack of attention to the relationship of school knowledge to extra school phenomena.

A fundamental starting point in these investigations has been best articulated by Michael F. D. Young when he notes that there is a "dialectical relationship between access to power and the opportunity to legitimize certain dominant categories, and the process by which the availability of such categories to some groups enables them to assert power and control over others." [4] In essence, just as there is a relatively unequal distribution of economic capital in society, so too is there a similar system of distribution surrounding cultural capital.[5] In advanced

[2] Herbert Gintis and Samuel Bowles. "The Contradictions of Liberal Educational Reform." In: Walter Feinberg and Henry Rosemont, Jr., editors, *Work, Technology, and Education.* Urbana: University of Illinois Press, 1975. p. 109.

[3] That this is not merely an "intellectual" interest, but embodies social and ideological commitments is examined in greater depth in: Michael W. Apple. "The Adequacy of Systems Management Procedures in Education." In: Ralph H. Smith, editor. *Regaining Educational Leadership.* New York: John Wiley and Sons, 1975.

[4] Michael F. D. Young. "Knowledge and Control." In: Michael F. D. Young, editor. *Knowledge and Control.* London: Collier-Macmillan Publishers, 1971. p. 8.

[5] John Kennett. "The Sociology of Pierre Bourdieu." *Educational Review* 25: 238; June 1973.

industrial societies, schools become particularly important as distributors of this cultural capital and play a critical role in giving legitimacy to categories and forms of knowledge. The very fact that certain traditions and normative "content" are construed as school knowledge is prima facie evidence of their perceived legitimacy.

We would like to argue here that the *problem* of educational knowledge, of what is taught in schools, has to be looked at as a form of the larger distribution of goods and services in a society. The study of educational knowledge is a study in ideology, the investigation of what is considered *legitimate* knowledge by specific social groups and classes, in specific institutions, at specific historical moments. In clearer terms, the overt and covert knowledge found within school settings and the principles of selection, organization, and evaluation of this knowledge are valuative selections from a much larger universe of possible knowledge and collection principles. Hence, they must not be accepted as given, but must be made problematic—bracketed, if you will—so that the social and economic ideologies, the institutionally patterned meanings, that stand behind them can be scrutinized. It is the latent meaning, the configuration that lies behind the commonsense acceptability of a position, that may be its most important attribute. And these hidden institutional meanings and relations [6] are almost never uncovered if we are guided only by amelioration.

As Kallos has noted in a recent paper, there are both manifest and latent "functions" of any educational system. These functions need to be characterized not only in educational (or learning) terms but, more important, in politico-economic terms. In short, discussions about the quality of educational life are relatively meaningless if the "specific functions of the educational system are unrecognized." [7] If much of the literature on what schools tacitly teach is accurate, then the specific functions may be more economic than "intellectual."

In this paper, we would like to focus on certain aspects of the problem of schooling and social and economic meaning. We shall look at schools as institutions that embody collective traditions and human intentions that are the products of identifiable social and economic ideologies. Thus, our basic starting point might best be phrased as a question, "*Whose* meanings are collected and distributed through the overt and hidden curricula in schools?" That is, as Marx was fond of saying,

[6] On the necessity of seeing institutions relationally, see: Bertell Ollman. *Alienation: Marx's Conception of Man in Capitalist Society.* New York: Cambridge University Press, 1971.

[7] Daniel Kallos. "Educational Phenomena and Educational Research." Report from the Institute of Education. University of Lund, Lund, Sweden. p. 7.

reality does not stalk around with a label. The curriculum in schools responds to and represents ideological and cultural resources that come from somewhere. Not all groups' visions are represented and not all groups' meanings are responded to. How, then, do schools act to distribute this cultural capital? Whose reality "stalks" in the corridors and classrooms of American schools?

We shall focus on two areas: First, we shall offer a description of the historical process through which certain social meanings became particularly *school* meanings, and thus now have the weight of decades of acceptance behind them. Second, we shall offer empirical evidence of a study of kindergarten experience to document the potency and staying power of these particular social meanings. Finally, we shall raise the question of whether piecemeal reforms, be they humanistically oriented or otherwise, can succeed.

Now the task of dealing with sets of meanings in schools has traditionally fallen upon the curriculum specialist. Historically, however, this concern for meanings in schools by curriculists has been linked to varied notions of social control. This should not surprise us. It should be obvious, though it is usually not so, that questions about meanings in social institutions tend to become questions of control.[8] That is, the forms of knowledge one finds within school settings—both overt and covert kinds of knowledge—imply relations of power and economic resources and control. The very choice of school knowledge, the act of designing school environments, though it may not be done consciously, often is based on ideological and economic presuppositions that provide the commonsense rules for educators' thought and action. Perhaps the linkages between meaning and control in schools can be made clear if we turn to a relatively abbreviated account of curricular history.

Meaning and Control in Curricular History

The British sociologist Bill Williamson argues that men and women "have to contend with the institutional and ideological forms of earlier times as the basic constraints on what they can achieve."[9] If one takes this notion seriously in looking at education, what is both provided and taught in schools must be understood historically. As he notes, "Earlier

[8] Dennis Warwick. "Ideologies, Integration, and Conflicts of Meaning." In: Michael Flude and John Ahier, editors. *Educability, Schools and Ideology.* London: Halstead Press, 1974. p. 94. See, also: Michael W. Apple. "Curriculum as Ideological Selection." *Comparative Education Review* 20:209-16; June 1976.

[9] Bill Williamson. "Continuities and Discontinuities in the Sociology of Education." In: Flude and Ahier, *op. cit.*, pp. 10-11.

educational attitudes of dominant groups in society still carry historical weight and are exemplified even in the bricks and mortar of the school buildings themselves." [10]

If we are to be honest with ourselves, the curriculum field itself has its roots in the soil of social control. From its very beginnings in the early part of this century when its intellectual paradigm took shape and became an identifiable set of procedures for selecting and organizing school knowledge, a set that should be taught to teachers and other educators, the fundamental consideration of the formative members of the curriculum field was that of social control. Part of this concern for social control is understandable. Many historically important figures who influenced the curriculum field (such as Charles C. Peters, Ross Finney, and especially David Snedden) had interests that spanned both the field of educational sociology and the more general problem of what should concretely happen in school. Given the growing importance of the idea of social control in the American Sociological Society at the time, an idea which seemed to capture both the imagination and energy of so many of the nation's intelligentsia, as well as powerful segments of the business community, it is not difficult to see how it also captured those figures who wore two hats, who were both sociologists and curriculum workers.[11]

But an interest in schooling as a mechanism for social control was not merely borrowed from sociology. The individuals who first called themselves curriculists (Franklin Bobbitt and W. W. Charters, for instance) were vitally concerned with social control for ideological reasons as well. Influenced strongly by the scientific management movement and the work of social measurement specialists,[12] and guided by beliefs that found the popular eugenics movement a "progressive" social force, these individuals brought social control into the very heart of the field whose task it was to develop criteria for selecting those meanings students would come into contact with in our educational institutions. . . .

For these people, education in general and the everyday meanings of the curriculum in schools in particular were seen as essential elements

10 *Ibid.*

11 Barry Franklin. "The Curriculum Field and the Problem of Social Control, 1918-1938: A Study in Critical Theory." Unpublished doctoral dissertation, The University of Wisconsin, Madison, 1974. pp. 2-3.

12 *Ibid.*, pp. 4-5. It should be noted here that scientific management itself was not necessarily a neutral technology for creating more efficient institutions. It was developed as a mechanism for the further division and control of labor. This is provocatively portrayed in: Harry Braverman. *Labor and Monopoly Capital: The Degradation of Work in the Twentieth Century.* New York: Monthly Review Press, 1975.

in the preservation of the existing social privilege, interests, and knowledge of one element of the population at the expense of less powerful groups.[13] Most often this took the form of attempting to guarantee expert and scientific control in society, to eliminate or "socialize" unwanted racial or ethnic groups of characteristics, or to produce an economically efficient group or citizens in order to, as C. C. Peters put it, reduce the maladjustment of workers to their jobs. It is this latter interest, the economic substratum of everyday school life, that will become of particular importance when we look at what schools teach about work and play in a later section of this essay.

Of course, neither the idea of nor an interest in social control emerged newborn through the early curriculum movement's attempts to use school knowledge for rather conservative social ends. Social control was an implied aim of a substantial number of ameliorative social and political programs carried out during the 19th century by both state and private agencies, so that order and stability, and the imperative of industrial growth, might be maintained in the face of a variety of social and economic changes.[14] As Feinberg's analysis of the ideological roots of liberal educational policy demonstrates even in this century many of the proposed "reforms" in schools and elsewhere latently served conservative social interests of stability and social stratification.[15]

The argument presented so far is not meant to debunk the efforts of educators and social reformers. Instead, it is an attempt to place the current argumentation over the "lack of humaneness in schools," the tacit teaching of social norms, values, and so forth, within a larger historical context. Without such a context we cannot fully understand the relationship between what schools actually do and an advanced industrial economy like our own. The best example of this context can be found in the changing ideological functions of schooling in general and curricular meanings in particular. Behind much of the argumentation about the role of formal education during the 19th century in the United States were a variety of concerns about the standardization of educational environments, the teaching through day to day school interaction of moral, normative, and dispositional values, and an economic functionalism. Today these concerns have been given the name of the hidden curriculum by Philip Jackson [16] and others. But it is the very question of its

---

[13] Ibid.

[14] Ibid., p. 317.

[15] Walter Feinberg. Reason and Rhetoric: The Intellectual Foundations of Twentieth Century Liberal Educational Policy. New York: John Wiley & Sons, 1975.

[16] Philip Jackson. Life in Classrooms. New York: Holt, Rinehart and Winston, 1968.

hiddenness that may help us uncover the historical relationship between what is taught in schools and the larger context of institutions which surround them.

We should be aware that historically the hidden curriculum was *not* hidden at all, but instead was the overt function of schools during much of their career as an institution. During the 19th century, the increasing diversity of political, social, and cultural attributes and structures "pushed educators to resume with renewed vigor the language of social control and homogenization that had dominated educational rhetoric from the earliest colonial period." [17] As the century progressed, the rhetoric of reform, of justifying one's ideological position against other interest groups, did not merely focus on the critical need for social homogeneity. Using schools as a primary agency for inculcating values, to create an "American community," was not enough. The growing pressures of modernization and industrialization also created certain expectations of efficiency and functionalism among certain classes and an industrial elite in society as well. As Vallance puts it, "to assertive socialization was added a focus on organizational efficiency." Thus, the reforms having the greatest effect on school organization and ultimately the procedures and principles which governed life in classrooms were dominated by the language of and an interest in production, well adjusted economic functioning, and bureaucratic skills. In this process the underlying reasons for reform slowly changed from an active concern for valuative consensus to an economic functionalism.[18] But this could only occur if the prior period, with its search for a standardized national character built in large part through the characteristics of schools, had been both accepted and perceived as successful. Thus, the institutional outlines of schools, the relatively standardized day to day forms of interaction, provided the mechanisms by which a normative consensus could be "taught." And within these broad outlines, these behavioral regularities of the institution if you will, an ideological set of commonsense rules for curriculum selection and organizing school experience based on efficiency, economic functionalism, and bureaucratic exigencies took hold. The former became the deep structure, the first hidden curriculum, which encased the latter. Once the hidden curriculum could become hidden, when a uniform and standardized learning context had become established and when social selection and control were taken as

[17] Elizabeth Vallance. "Hiding the Hidden Curriculum." *Curriculum Theory Network* 4: 15; Fall 1973-74.
[18] *Ibid.*

given in schooling, only then could attention be paid to the needs of the individual or other more "ethereal" concerns.[19]

Thus, historically, built into the very structure of formal education was a core of commonsense meanings combining normative consensus and economic adjustment. This is not to say that there have been no significant educational movements toward, say, education for self-development. Rather, it argues that behind these preferential choices about individual needs there was a more powerful set of expectations surrounding schooling that provided the constitutive structure of school experience. As a number of economists have recently noted, the most economically important "latent function" of school life seems to be the selection and generation of personality attributes and normative meanings that enable one to have a supposed chance at economic rewards.[20] Since the school is the only major institution that stands between the family and the labor market, it is not odd that both historically and currently certain social meanings that have differential benefits are distributed in schools.

But what are these particular social meanings? How are they organized and displayed in everyday school life? It is these questions to which we shall now turn.

Ideology and Curriculum-in-Use

The larger concerns with the relationship between ideology and school knowledge, between meaning and control, of the prior section tend to be altogether too vague unless one can see them as active forces in the' activity of school people and students as they go about their particular lives in classrooms. As investigators of the hidden curriculum and others have noted, the concrete modes by which knowledge is distributed in classrooms and the commonsense practices of teachers and students can illuminate the connection between school life and the structures of ideology, power, and economic resources of which schools are a part.[21]

[19] *Ibid.*, pp. 18-19.

[20] Bowles and Gintis, *op. cit.*, p. 133. These normative meanings and personality attributes are distributed unequally to different "types" of students, often by social class or occupational expectation, as well. Not all students get the same dispositional elements nor are the same meanings attached to them by the distributor of cultural capital. See: Bowles and Gintis, *op. cit.*, p. 136.

[21] See, for example: Michael W. Apple. "Ivan Illich and Deschooling Society: The Politics of Slogan Systems." In: Nobuo Shimahara and Adam Scrupski, editors. *Social Forces and Schooling.* New York: David McKay, 1975. pp. 337-60; and Michael F. D. Young. "An Approach to the Study of Curricula as Socially Organized Knowledge." In: Young, *Knowledge and Control, op. cit.*, pp. 19-46.

Just as there is a social distribution of cultural capital in society, so too is there a social distribution of knowledge within classrooms. For example, different "kinds" of students get different kinds of knowledge, as Keddie so well documents in her study of the knowledge teachers have of their students and the curricular knowledge then made available to them.[22] However, while the differential distribution of classroom knowledge does exist and is intimately linked to the process of social labeling that goes on in schools,[23] it is less important to our own analysis here than what might be called the "deep structure" of school experience. What are the underlying meanings that are negotiated and transmitted in schools behind the actual formal "stuff" of curriculum content? What happens when knowledge is filtered through teachers? Through what categories of normality and deviance is it filtered? What is the *basic and organizing framework* of the normative and conceptual knowledge that students do actually get? In short, what is the *curriculum-in-use?* It is only by seeing this deep structure that we can begin pointing out how social norms, institutions, and ideological rules are ongoingly sustained by the day to day interaction of commonsense actors as they go about their normal practices.[24] This is especially true in classrooms. Social definitions about school knowledge, definitions that are both dialectically related to and rest within the larger context of the surrounding social and economic institutions, are maintained and recreated by the commonsense practices of teaching and evaluation in classrooms.[25]

We shall focus on kindergarten here because it occupies a critical moment in the process by which students become competent in the rules, norms, values, and dispositions "necessary" to function within institutional life as it now exists. Learning the role of student is a complex activity, one that takes time and continual interaction with institutional expectations. By focusing on both how this occurs and the content of the dispositions that are both overtly and covertly part of kindergarten

[22] Nell Keddie. "Classroom Knowledge." In: Young, *Knowledge and Control, op. cit.*, pp. 133-60.

[23] Michael Apple. "Common Sense Categories and Curriculum Thought." In: James B. Macdonald and Esther Zaret, editors. *Schools in Search of Meaning.* Washington, D.C.: Association for Supervision and Curriculum Development, 1975. pp. 116-48.

[24] This, of course, is a fundamental tenet of ethnomethodological studies, as well. See: Peter McHugh. *Defining the Situation.* Indianapolis: Bobbs-Merrill Co., 1968; Roy Turner, editor. *Ethnomethodology.* Baltimore: Penguin Books, 1974; and Aaron Cicourel. *Cognitive Sociology.* New York: The Free Press, 1974.

[25] For further explication of this point, see: Basil Berstein. "On the Classification and Framing of Educational Knowledge." In: Michael F. D. Young, *Knowledge and Control, op. cit.*, pp. 47-69.

knowledge, we can begin to illuminate the background knowledge children use as organizing principles for much of the rest of their school career.

In short, the social definitions internalized during one's initial school life provide the constitutive rules for later life in classrooms. Thus what is construed as work or play, "school knowledge" or merely "my knowledge," normality or deviance, are the elements that need to be looked at. As we shall see, the use of praise, rules of access to materials, the control of both time and emotionality all make significant contributions to teaching social meanings in school. But as we shall also see it is the meanings attached to the category of work that most clearly illuminate the possible place of schools in the complex nexus of economic and social institutions which surround us all.

Kindergarten experience serves as a foundation for the years of schooling which follow. Children who have attended kindergarten tend to demonstrate a general superiority in achievement in the elementary grades over children who have not attended kindergarten. However, attempts to determine exactly which teaching techniques and learning experiences contribute most directly to the "intellectual and emotional growth" of kindergarten children have produced inconclusive results. Kindergarten training appears to exert its most powerful and lasting influence on the attitudes and the behavior of the children by acclimating them to a classroom environment. Children are introduced to their roles as elementary school pupils in kindergarten classrooms; it is the understanding and mastery of this *role* which makes for the greater success of kindergarten-trained children in elementary school.

Socialization in kindergarten classrooms includes the learning of norms and definitions of social interactions. It is the ongoing development of a working definition of the situation by the participants. In order to function adequately in a social situation, those involved must reach a common understanding of the meanings, limitations, and potential the setting affords for their interaction. During the first few weeks of the school year, the children and the teacher forge a common definition of the situation out of repeated interaction in the classroom. When one common set of social meanings is accepted, classroom activities will proceed smoothly.[26] . . .

Of course, teachers are not free to define the classroom situation in

---

[26] Socialization is not only a one way process, of course. See: Robert MacKay. "Conceptions of Children and Models of Socialization." In: Hans Peter Drietzel, editor. *Childhood and Socialization.* New York: Macmillan Publishing Co., 1973. pp. 27-43.

any way they choose. As we saw earlier in this paper, the school is a well-established institution, and it may be that neither the teacher nor the children can perceive more than marginal ways to deviate to any significant degree from the commonsense rules and expectations which make school school and not some other institution.

The negotiation of meanings in a kindergarten classroom is a critical phase in the socialization of the children. The meanings of classroom objects and events are not intrinsic to them, but are formed through social interaction. . . . These meanings become clear to the children as they participate in the social setting. The *use* of materials, the nature of authority, the quality of personal relationships, the spontaneous remarks, as well as other aspects of daily classroom life contribute to the child's growing awareness of his or her role in the classroom and his or her understanding of the social setting. Therefore, to understand the social reality of schooling it is necessary to study it in actual classroom settings. Each concept, role, and object is a social creation bound to the situation in which it is produced. The meanings of classroom interaction cannot be assumed; they must be discovered. The abstraction of these meanings and the generalizations and insights drawn from them may be applicable to other contexts, but the researcher's initial descriptions, understandings, and interpretations require that the social phenomena be encountered where they are produced, that is, in the classroom.[27]

Observation and interviewing of the participants in one particular public school kindergarten classroom revealed that the social meanings of events and materials are established remarkably early in the school year. As with most classroom settings, the socialization of the children was an overt priority during the opening weeks of school. The four most important skills the teacher expected the children to learn during those opening weeks were to share, to listen, to put things away, and to follow the classroom routine. Thus, her statement of her goals for the children's early school experiences also constitutes her definition of socialized behavior in the classroom.

The children had little part in organizing the classroom materials and were relatively impotent to affect the course of daily events. The

[27] An excellent treatment of this "ethnographic" tradition can be found in: Philip E. D. Robinson. "An Ethnography of Classrooms." In: John Eggleston, editor. *Contemporary Research in the Sociology of Education.* London: Methuen and Co., 1974. pp. 251-66. For further discussion of this methodological issue, and for further empirical data on which the findings reported here are based, see: Nancy R. King. "The Hidden Curriculum and the Socialization of Kindergarten Children." Unpublished doctoral dissertation, The University of Wisconsin, Madison, 1976.

teacher made no special effort to make the children comfortable in the room, or to reduce their uncertainty about the schedule of activities. Rather than mediating intrusive aspects of the environment, she chose to require that the children accommodate themselves to the materials as presented. When the ongoing noise of another class in the hallway distracted the children, for example, the teacher called for their attention, but she did not close the door. Similarly, the cubbies where the children kept their crayons, smocks, and tennis shoes were not labeled although the children had considerable difficulty remembering which cubby they had been assigned. In spite of many instances of lost crayons and crying children, the teacher refused to permit the student teacher to label the cubbies. She told the student teacher that the children must learn to remember their assigned cubbies because "that is their job." When one girl forget where her cubby was on the day after they had been assigned, the teacher pointed her out to the class as an example of a "girl who was not listening yesterday."

The objects in the classroom were attractively displayed in an apparent invitation to the class to interact with them. Most of the materials were placed on the floor or on shelves within easy reach of the children. However, the opportunities to interact with materials in the classroom were severely circumscribed. The teacher's organization of time in the classroom contradicted the apparent availability of materials in the physical setting. During most of the kindergarten session, the children were not permitted to handle objects. The materials, then, were organized so that the children learned restraint; they learned to handle things within easy reach only when permitted to do so by the teacher. The children were "punished" for touching things when the time was not right and praised for the moments when they were capable of restraint. For example, the teacher praised the children for their prompt obedience when they quickly stopped bouncing basketballs when told to do so in the gym. She made no mention of their ball handling skills.

The teacher made it clear to the children that good kindergarteners were quiet and cooperative. One morning a child brought two large stuffed dolls to school and sat them in her assigned seat. During the first period of large group instruction, the teacher referred to them saying, "Raggedy Ann and Raggedy Andy are such good helpers! They haven't said a thing all morning."

As part of learning to exhibit socialized behavior the children learned to tolerate ambiguity and discomfort in the classroom and to accept a considerable degree of arbitrariness in their school activities. They were required to adjust their emotional responses to conform to those considered appropriate by the teacher. They learned to respond to her personally and to the manner in which she organized the classroom environment.

After some two weeks of kindergarten experience, the children had established a category system for defining and organizing their social reality in the classroom. Their interview responses indicated that the activities in the classroom did not have intrinsic meanings; the children assigned meanings depending on the context in which each was carried on. The teacher presented the classroom materials either as a part of instruction, or more overtly, she discussed and demonstrated their uses to the class. This is a critical point. The use of a particular object, that is, the manner in which we are predisposed to act toward it, constitutes its meaning for us. In defining the meanings of the things in the classroom, then, the teacher defined the nature of the relationships between the children and the materials with contextual meanings bound to the classroom environment.

When asked about classroom objects, the children responded with remarkable agreement and uniformity. The children divided the materials into two categories: things to work with and things to play with. No child organized any material in violation of what seemed to be their guiding principle. Those materials which the children used at the direction of the teacher were work materials. These included books, paper, paste, crayons, glue, and other materials traditionally associated with school tasks. No child chose to use these materials during "play" time early in the school year. The materials which the children chose during free time were labeled play materials or toys. These materials included, among other things, games, small manipulatives, the playhouse, dolls, and the wagon.

The meaning of classroom materials, then, is derived from the nature of the activity in which they are used. The categories of work and play emerged as powerful organizers of the classroom reality early in the school year. Both the teacher and the children considered work activities more important than play activities. Information which the children said they learned in school was all things that the teacher had told them during activities they called "work." "Play" activities were permitted only if time allowed, and the children had finished the assigned work activities. Observation data revealed that the category of work has several well-defined parameters which sharply separate it from the category of play. First, work includes any and all teacher-directed activities; only free time activities were called "play" by the children. Activities such as coloring, drawing, waiting in line, listening to stories, watching movies, cleaning up, and singing were called work. To work, then, is to do what one is *told* to do, no matter the nature of the activity involved.

Second, all work activities, and only work activities, were compulsory. For example, the children were required to draw pictures about specific topics on numerous occasions. During singing the teacher often interrupted to encourage and exhort the children who were not singing or singing too softly. Any choices that were permitted during work periods were circumscribed to fit the limits of accepted uniform procedure. During an Indian dance, for example, the teacher allowed the "sleeping" children to snore if they wanted. After a trip to the fire station all of the children were required to draw a picture, but each child was permitted to choose whatever part of the tour he/she liked best as the subject of the picture. (Of course it is also true that each child was required to illustrate his/her favorite part of the trip.) When introducing another art project the teacher said, "Today you will make a cowboy horse. You can make your horse any color you want, black or grey, or brown." At another time she announced with great emphasis that the children could choose three colors for the flowers they were making from cupcake liners. The children gasped with excitement and applauded. These choices did not change the principle that the children were required to use the same materials in the same manner during work periods. If anything, the nature of the choices emphasized the general principle.

Not only was every work activity required, but every child had to start at the designated time. The entire class worked on all assigned tasks simultaneously. Further, all of the children were required to complete the assigned tasks during the designated work period. In a typical incident, on the second day of school, many children complained that they either could not or did not want to finish a lengthy art project. The teacher said that everyone must finish. One child asked if she could finish "next time," but the teacher replied, "You must finish now."

In addition to requiring that all the children do the same thing at the same time, work activities also involved the children with the same materials and produced similar or identical products or attainments. During work periods the same materials were presented to the entire class simultaneously, and the same product was expected of each of the children. All of the children were expected to use work materials in the same way. Even seemingly inconsequential procedures had to be followed by every child. For example, after large group instruction on the second day of school, the teacher told the children, "Get a piece of paper and your crayons, and go back to your seats." One child, who got her crayons first, was reminded to get her paper first.

The products or skills which the children exhibited at the completion of a period of work were supposed to be similar or identical. The teacher demonstrated most art projects to the entire class before the children got their materials. The children then tried to produce a product as similar to the one the teacher had made as possible. Only those pieces of art work which were nearly identical to the product the teacher made as demonstration were saved and displayed in the classroom.

Work periods, as defined by the children, then, involved every child simultaneously in the same directed activity with the same materials to the same ends. The point of work activities was to *do* them, not necessarily to do them well. By the second day of school, many children hastily finished their assigned tasks in order to join their friends playing with toys. During music, for example, the teacher exhorted the children to sing loudly. Neither tunefulness, rhythm, nor purity of tone and mood were mentioned to the children, or expected of them. It was their enthusiastic and lusty participation which was required. Similarly, the teacher accepted any child's art project upon which sufficient time had been spent. The assigned tasks were compulsory and identical, and, in accepting all finished products, the teacher often accepted poor and/or shoddy work. The acceptance of such work nullified the notion of excellence as an evaluative category. Diligence, perseverance, obedience, and participation were rewarded. These are behaviors of the children, not characteristics of their work. In this way the notion of excellence became separated from the concept of successful or acceptable work and was replaced by the criteria of adequate participation.

The children interviewed in September, and again in October, used the categories of work and play to create and describe their social reality. Their responses indicate that the first few weeks of school are an important time for learning about the nature of work in the classroom. In September no child said "work" when asked what children do in kindergarten. In October half of those interviewed responded with the word "work." All of the children talked more about working and less about playing in October than they had in September. The teacher was pleased with the progress of the class during the first weeks of school and repeatedly referred to the children as "my good workers."

The teacher often justified her presentation of work activities in the classroom in terms of the preparation of the children for elementary school and for adulthood. For example, she believed that work activities should be compulsory because the children needed practice following directions without exercising options as preparation for the reality of adult work. The children were expected to view kindergarten as a year of preparation for the first grade. In stressing the importance of coloring neatly or sequencing pictures properly, the teacher spoke of the necessity of these skills in first grade, and the difficulty children who were inattentive in kindergarten would have the following year.

Thus, as part of their initiation into the kindergarten community, young children also receive their first initiation into the social dimension of the world of work. The content of specific lessons is relatively less important than the experience of being a worker. Personal attributes of obedience, enthusiasm, adaptability, and perseverance are more highly valued than academic competence. Unquestioning acceptance of authority and the vicissitudes of life in institutional settings are among a kindergartener's first lessons. It is in the progressive acceptance as natural, as the world "tout court," of meanings of important and unimportant knowledge, of work and play, of normality and deviance, that these lessons reside.

Beyond a Rhetorical Humanism

As the late Italian social theorist Antonio Gramsci argued, the control of the knowledge preserving and producing sectors of a society becomes a critical factor in enhancing the ideological dominance of one group of people or class over less powerful groups of people or classes.[28] In this regard, the role of the school in selecting, preserving, and passing on conceptions of competence, ideological norms and values, and often only certain social groups' "knowledge"—all of which are embedded within both the overt and hidden curricula in schools—is of no small moment.

At least two aspects of school life serve rather interesting distributive social and economic functions. As the growing literature on the hidden curriculum shows and as we have offered historical and empirical evidence here, the forms of interaction in school life may serve as mechanisms for communicating normative and dispositional meanings to students. Yet the body of school knowledge itself—what is included and excluded, what is important and what is unimportant—also often serves an ideological purpose.

As one of this paper's authors has demonstrated in an earlier analysis, much of the formal content of curricular knowledge is dominated by a consensus ideology. Conflict, either intellectual or normative,

[28] Thomas R. Bates. "Gramsci and the Theory of Hegemony." *Journal of the History of Ideas* 36: 360; April-June 1975.

is seen as a negative attribute in social life.[29] Thus there is a peculiar kind of redundancy in school knowledge. Both the everyday experience and the curricular knowledge itself display messages of normative and cognitive consensus. The deep structure of school life, the basic and organizing framework of commonsense rules that is negotiated, internalized, and ultimately seems to give meaning to our experience in educational institutions, seems closely linked to the normative and communicative structures of industrial life.[30] How could it be otherwise?

Perhaps we can expect little more from the school experience than what we have portrayed here given the distribution of resources in the United States and given the wishes of a large portion of the citizenry. One hypothesis that should not be dismissed too readily, in fact, is that schools do work. In an odd way, they may succeed in reproducing a population that is roughly equivalent to the economic and social stratification in society. Thus, when one asks of schools, "Where is their humaneness?," perhaps the answers may be more difficult to grapple with than the questioner expects.

For example, one could interpret this essay as a statement against a particular community's commitment to education or as a negative statement about particular kinds of teachers who are "less able than they might be." This would be basically incorrect, we believe. The city is educationally oriented. It spends a large amount of its resources on schooling and feels that it deserves its reputation as having one of the best school systems in the area, if not the nation.

Just as important, we should be careful not to view this kind of teacher as poorly trained, unsuccessful, or uncaring. Exactly the opposite is often the case. The classroom teacher who was observed is, in fact, perceived as a competent teacher by administrators, colleagues, and parents. Given this, the teacher's activities must be understood not merely in terms of the patterns of social interaction that dominate classrooms, but in terms of the wider patterning of social and economic relationships in the social structure of which he or she and the school itself are a part.[31]

29 Michael W. Apple. "The Hidden Curriculum and the Nature of Conflict." *Interchange* 2 (4): 29-40; 1971.

30 Habermas' arguments about patterns of communicative competence in advanced industrial "orders" are quite interesting as interpretive schema here. See, for example: Jurgen Habermas. "Towards a Theory of Communicative Competence." In: Hans Peter Drietzel, editor. *Recent Sociology*. No. 2. New York: The Macmillan Co., 1970. pp. 115-48; and Trent Schroyer. *The Critique of Domination*. New York: George Braziller, 1973.

31 Rachel Sharp and Anthony Green. *Education and Social Control: A Study in Progressive Primary Education*. Boston: Routledge and Kegan Paul, 1975. p. 8.

When teachers distribute normative interpretations of, say, work and play like the ones we have documented historically and currently here, one must ask "to what problems are these viable solutions for the teacher?"[32] "What is the commonsense interpretive framework of teachers and to what set of ideological presuppositions does it respond?" In this way we can situate classroom knowledge and activity within the larger framework of structural relationships which—either through teacher and parent expectations, the classroom material environment, what are considered important problems for teachers to focus on, or the relationship between schools and, say, the economic sector of a society—often determine what goes on in classrooms.

This paper by itself cannot totally support the argument that schools seem to act latently to enhance an already unequal and stratified social order. It does confirm, however, a number of recent analyses that point out how schools, through their distribution of a number of social and ideological categories, contribute to the promotion of a rather static framework of institutions.[33] Thus, our argument should not be seen as a statement against an individual school or any particular group of teachers. Rather, we want to suggest that educators need to see teachers as "encapsulated" within a social and economic context that by necessity often produces the problems teachers are confronted with and the material limitations on their responses. This very "external" context provides substantial legitimation for the allocation of teachers' time and energies[34] and for the kinds of cultural capital embodied in the school itself.

If this is the case, as we strongly suggest it is, the questions we ask must go beyond the humanistic level (without losing their humanistic and emancipatory intent) to a more relational approach.[35] While educators continue to ask what is wrong in schools and what can be done—can our problems be "solved" with more humanistic teachers, more openness, better content, and so on—it is of immense import that we begin to take seriously the questions of "In whose interest do schools often function today?" and "What is the relation between the distribution of cultural capital and economic capital?" And, finally, "Can we deal with the political and economic realities of creating institutions which enhance meaning and lessen control?" . . .

[32] *Ibid.*, p. 13.

[33] *Ibid.*, p. 110-12. See, also: the provocative analysis found in Basil Bernstein. *Class, Codes, and Control. Volume III: Towards a Theory of Educational Transmissions.* Boston: Routledge and Kegan Paul, 1975.

[34] *Ibid.*, p. 116.

[35] *Ibid.*, p. x.

Thus, to isolate school experience from the complex totality of which it is a constitutive part is to be a bit too limited in one's analysis. In fact, the study of the relationship between ideology and school knowledge is especially important for our understanding of the larger social collectivity of which we are all a part. It enables us to begin to see how a society reproduces itself, how it perpetuates its conditions of existence through the selection and transmission of certain kinds of cultural capital upon which a complex yet unequal industrial society depends, and how it maintains cohesion among its classes and individuals by propagating ideologies that ultimately sanction the existing institutional arrangements which may cause the unnecessary stratification and inequality in the first place.[36] Can we afford not to understand these things?

[36] *Ibid.*, p. 221.

Contributors to This Book

Michael W. Apple, Professor of Curriculum and Instruction, University of Wisconsin, Madison

Wililam E. Doll, Jr., Associate Professor of Education, State University of New York, Oswego

Walter Doyle, Associate Professor of Education, North Texas State University, Denton

Daniel L. Duke, Professor of Teacher Education, Stanford University, Stanford, California

Dwayne Huebner, Professor of Education, Teachers College, Columbia University, New York

Nancy R. King, Assistant Professor of Education, Wheelock College, Boston

Charles A. Letteri, Director, Center for Cognitive Studies, University of Vermont, Burlington

James B. Macdonald, Distinguished Professor of Education, University of North Carolina, Greensboro

Alex Molnar, *Editor;* Assistant Professor of Education, University of Wisconsin, Milwaukee

Gerald Ponder, Associate Professor of Education, North Texas State University, Denton

Elizabeth S. Randolph, Assistant Superintendent, Zone II, Charlotte-Mecklenburg Schools, Charlotte, North Carolina

Ralph W. Tyler, Director Emeritus, Center for Advanced Study in the Behavioral Sciences, University of Chicago, Chicago

Robert Allen Ubbelohde, Dean of Student Development and Associate Professor of Education, Earlham College, Richmond, Indiana

David C. Williams, Assistant Professor of Education, State University of New York, Albany

Bernice J. Wolfson, Chairperson, Department of Elementary and Early Childhood Education, University of Alabama, Birmingham

John A. Zahorik, *Editor;* Professor of Education, University of Wisconsin, Milwaukee

ASCD Publications, Autumn 1977

Yearbooks

Education for an Open Society (610-74012) $8.00

Education for Peace: Focus on Mankind (610-17946) $7.50

Evaluation as Feedback and Guide (610-17700) $6.50

Feeling, Valuing, and the Art of Growing: Insights into the Affective (610-77104) $9.75

Freedom, Bureaucracy, & Schooling (610-17508) $6.50

Learning and Mental Health in the School (610-17674) $5.00

Life Skills in School and Society (610-17786) $5.50

A New Look at Progressive Education (610-17812) $8.00

Perspectives on Curriculum Development 1776-1976 (610-76078) $9.50

Schools in Search of Meaning (610-75044) $8.50

Perceiving, Behaving, Becoming: A New Focus for Education (610-17278) $5.00

To Nurture Humaneness: Commitment for the '70's (610-17810) $6.00

Books and Booklets

Action Learning: Student Community Service Projects (611-74018) $2.50

Adventuring, Mastering, Associating: New Strategies for Teaching Children (611-76080) $5.00

Beyond Jencks: The Myth of Equal Schooling (611-17928) $2.00

The Changing Curriculum: Mathematics (611-17724) $2.00

Criteria for Theories of Instruction (611-17756) $2.00

Curricular Concerns in a Revolutionary Era (611-17852) $6.00

Curriculum Leaders: Improving Their Influence (611-76084) $4.00

Curriculum Theory (611-77112) $7.00

Degrading the Grading Myths: A Primer of Alternatives to Grades and Marks (611-76082) $6.00

Differentiated Staffing (611-17924) $3.50

Discipline for Today's Children and Youth (611-17314) $1.50

Educational Accountability: Beyond Behavioral Objectives (611-17856) $2.50

Elementary School Mathematics: A Guide to Current Research (611-75056) $5.00

Elementary School Science: A Guide to Current Research (611-17726) $2.25

Eliminating Ethnic Bias in Instructional Materials: Comment and Bibliography (611-74020) $3.25

Emerging Moral Dimensions in Society: Implications for Schooling (611-75052) $3.75

Ethnic Modification of Curriculum (611-17832) $1.00

Global Studies: Problems and Promises for Elementary Teachers (611-76086) $4.50

The Humanities and the Curriculum (611-17708) $2.00

Impact of Decentralization on Curriculum: Selected Viewpoints (611-75050) $3.75

Improving Educational Assessment & An Inventory of Measures of Affective Behavior (611-17804) $4.50

International Dimension of Education (611-17816) $2.25

Interpreting Language Arts Research for the Teacher (611-17846) $4.00

Learning More About Learning (611-17310) $2.00

Linguistics and the Classroom Teacher (611-17720) $2.75

A Man for Tomorrow's World (611-17838) $2.25

Middle School in the Making (611-74024) $5.00

The Middle School We Need (611-75060) $2.50

Multicultural Education: Commitments, Issues, and Applications (611-77108) $7.00

Needs Assessment: A Focus for Curriculum Development (611-75048) $4.00

Observational Methods in the Classroom (611-17948) $3.50

Open Education: Critique and Assessment (611-75054) $4.75

Open Schools for Children (611-17916) $3.75

Professional Supervision for Professional Teachers (611-75046) $4.50

Removing Barriers to Humaneness in the High School (611-17848) $2.50

Reschooling Society: A Conceptual Model (611-17950) $2.00

The School of the Future—NOW (611-17920) $3.75

Schools Become Accountable: A PACT Approach (611-74016) $3.50

The School's Role as Moral Authority (611-77110) $4.50

Social Studies for the Evolving Individual (611-17952) $3.00

Staff Development: Staff Liberation (611-77106) $6.50

Supervision: Emerging Profession (611-17796) $5.00

Supervision in a New Key (611-17926) $2.50

Supervision: Perspectives and Propositions (611-17732) $2.00

What Are the Sources of the Curriculum? (611-17522) $1.50

Vitalizing the High School (611-74026) $3.50

Developmental Characteristics of Children and Youth (wall chart) (611-75058) $2.00

Discounts on quantity orders of same title to single address: 10-49 copies, 10%; 50 or more copies, 15%. Make checks or money orders payable to ASCD. Orders totaling $10.00 or less must be prepaid. Orders from institutions and businesses must be on official purchase order form. Shipping and handling charges will be added to billed purchase orders. **Please be sure to list the stock number of each publication, shown in parentheses.**

Subscription to **Educational Leadership**—$10.00 a year. ASCD Membership dues: Regular (subscription and yearbook)—$25.00 a year; Comprehensive (includes subscription and yearbook plus other books and booklets distributed during period of membership)—$35.00 a year.

Order from: **Association for Supervision and Curriculum Development Suite 1100, 1701 K Street, N.W., Washington, D.C. 20006**